Tom Snyder Productions

Great Teaching

in the

One Computer

Classroom

David A. Dockterman, Ed.D.

3rd EDITION

Includes Video, Videodisc & Multimedia

**Dedicated to great teachers, great classes,
and the pursuit of great education.**

The TSP Team
Tom Snyder, Richard Abrams, David Dockterman, Peter Reynolds, Annette Donnelly,
Sharon A. LeBoeuf, Althea Kaemmer, Christina McCartney, Nancy Bogosian,
Bruce Green, David G. O'Neil, Robert Thibeault, Annette LeBlanc Cate,
Robert C. Keough, Eytan Bernet, Kristen Keith, Jeanne Feehrer, Naomi Halpern,
Carl Adams, Rick Daneault, Andre Lyman, Greg Mardirosian,
Andrew B. Lizotte and Baldassarre Lolacono.

Copyright © 1989, 1990, 1991 by Tom Snyder Productions, Inc. All rights reserved. No part of this publication may be reproduced, stored in a retrieval system, or transmitted, in any form or by any means, electronic, mechanical, photocopying, recording, or otherwise, without the prior written permission of the publisher, except for pages 125-142, which may be copied for educational uses only.

LB
1028.46
.D43
1991

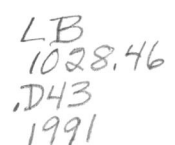

Contents

What is Great Teaching 4

About the Author 6

Preface 7

Introduction to The Third Edition 9

My Path to the One Computer Classroom 11

Let's Decide Where We're Going 25

A Tool for the Professional Teacher 37

The Computer as a Presentation Tool 55

The Computer as a Discussion Generator 73

The Computer and Cooperative Learning 83

Interactive Video, Multmedia, & All that Jazz 97

Notes from the Field 115

Some Aides for Sharing Ideas 124

Related Historical & Contemporary Reading .. 143

What is Great Teaching?
by Tom Snyder

If you ask 40 students from a liberal, east-coast graduate school of education to write 1 page about their most influential teacher, will the results be predictable? I did it, and they weren't.

I drew a ten foot line on the black board that was to represent a continuum of teaching styles described by these one page papers. After reading a paper aloud, we would attach that paper somewhere along the line, the left end reserved for the most open-ended teaching styles: student centered, discovery learning based, teacher as co-pilot in the voyage of learning. The right end of the line would be reserved for the most teacher-driven, autocratic, personality and charisma based teaching. After reading each page aloud, I then "walked the line", asking the class to vote for the most appropriate place to tape the writing to the board. So where were all the papers clustered when we had finished? Please guess before reading on...

This particular group of forty papers were distributed a smooth as silk over ten feet of imaginable styles. On the left were teachers from the seventies who let their students create their own collages/films/newspapers/solar collectors/geodesic this and thats. The right end of the line held accounts of passionate teachers who said, "give yourself fully to me for a semester or two and in return I will show you how to perceive a still-life, how to understand the flux of history, how Shakespeare can be felt deep in the heart." Across the middle of the line were spread all of the other heroes of teaching.

You could say that this particular continuum shows us that there is no one particular winning style. Or you could reasonably claim that this continuum produces no new understanding. More interesting would be a spectrum that crowded the cherished memories of students on one end. What would that spectrum be, we asked ourselves. Try a continuum that sails from **passionate** to **indifferent**, or from **willing to connect with students** to **personally inaccessible**. There, we thought, you will get agreement.

Reading the literature from the world of school technologies over the last decade, one gets the impression that the true heroic work of microprocessors will be to relieve us from the tyranny of teacher-centered learning. If this happens, we will be disappointing at least half of our students. The achievements of educational progressivism have been many. I, for one, owe my career to them. The failed aspects of progressivism have emasculated, diminished and subverted the intuitive efforts of many teachers. In England, recent studies of progressive classrooms have revealed teachers who spend far too much time apologizing for their intrusions. *Don't tell the kids the answers. OK. Don't even tell the kids the questions. OK. As a matter of fact, could you move out of the frame, please.* Sure, if that's what is best...

Passion, relationships, fascination, humanity, caring: some teachers will demonstrate the power of these from afar and some from on high. In the coming century we shall discover, and I only hope it does not take too long, that technology's job is to support their choice.

About the Author

David Dockterman received his B.A. in history and teaching certification at Yale University. He taught high school social studies and history for several years in Connecticut and received his Ed.D. from the Harvard Graduate School of Education in 1988. His thesis analyzed historical efforts to bring technological innovation into the classroom. Currently, David is a vice-president at Tom Snyder Productions. He co-designed and authored the simulations for both the *Decisions, Decisions*™ and *Choices, Choices*™ series of discussion-based software. In addition, David is the editor of *The Professional Teacher*, TSP's quarterly newsletter for educators.

Preface

Teaching in the One Computer Classroom expresses in concrete terms much of what we believe and hold dear at Tom Snyder Productions, and this book reflects our overriding commitment to improving the quality of education in our schools. The people who make up TSP are drawn together by a common philosophy, a vision of dynamic, interactive classrooms where students and teachers engage in the informed exploration of knowledge and ideas. That vision is our goal. We view the computer as one medium to help us reach it.

There are great classes out there in the world of schools — not enough of them, but they are there. They have been created through the exhausting efforts of teachers and administrators, parents and children, who also share this vision and commitment. These classes exist without the computer, but the technology can help them proliferate. This book offers specific ideas about how that can happen.

The computer can ease the administrative burden teachers face; it can spark and help manage incredible class discussions; it can take a group of students on a field trip to a faraway world without ever leaving the classroom; it can provide teachers with a more powerful "chalkboard" than they ever imagined; it can do all this and much more.

Our charter at Tom Snyder Productions is to create, discover, and promote computer applications that perform these tasks, that empower teachers to do more of what they do best: teach. We have had success with this charter because we understand the realities of the educational system, and our instincts about what works in the classroom remain intact. We empathize with teachers who view the computer through the same doubting eyes that watched open classrooms and educa-

A Message from Tom Snyder Productions

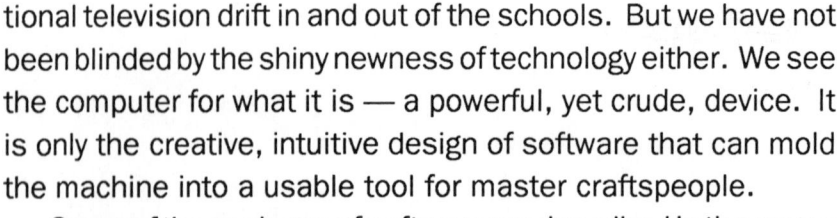

tional television drift in and out of the schools. But we have not been blinded by the shiny newness of technology either. We see the computer for what it is — a powerful, yet crude, device. It is only the creative, intuitive design of software that can mold the machine into a usable tool for master craftspeople.

Some of those pieces of software are described in the pages that follow. We offer you this book not in the hope that it will provide you with the ultimate "solution." Rather, we hope the ideas expressed here will help you begin to frame the right questions and guide you toward discovering your own answers. We want to help. And it is in that vein that Tom Snyder Productions seeks a partnership with you, with principals, with superintendents, and with all those who seek to foster quality education.

Introduction to the 3rd Edition

This is a book for teachers and those who work with teachers. I present it to you in the hope that, as teachers, you can identify with my experiences as a technological novice in the classroom and learn from them as I have. I have made an effort throughout these pages to maintain a loose, informal style. My digressions and stories (of which there are many) are meant to enlighten, to help you make connections to your own life in the classroom. So please be patient. My meanderings generally lead somewhere.

This third edition leaves the center of the book intact. I have only added to the edges. At the front edge you will find a letter from Tom Snyder. His words reinforce the emphasis in the title on Great Teaching. It's just another reminder that our goal is not more technology in schools, but marvelous teaching in all its wonderful forms.

Near the outer edge of the book I have added a chapter that expands the scope of the work beyond just computers. The recent wave of enthusiasm surrounding multimedia and video prompted me to tackle this new phase of the "interactive" revolution directly. I hope you find this addition valuable.

The remainder of the book remains unchanged. The first chapter describes through a bit of autobiography an evolution of ideas and the development of a philosophy of computer use in the classroom. I attempt in the second chapter to encourage your participation in the construction of a theoretical framework for considering the what is now five chapters that follow it. In these pages I discuss specific applications — some new, some old, but all readily accessible — representative of different classroom uses, from teacher productivity to cooperative learning. Within those applications, I hope you will find something that fits your particular needs. I also hope that you will share these ideas with your colleagues. The reproducible materials at the end of the book are placed there to help you do just that. My goal was to be both thoughtful and practical. I hope I come close.

My Path to the One Computer Classroom

This picture shows me in my classroom *before* the computer invasion. Well, it's not literally a "before" picture of me, but it conveys the basic idea: many kids sitting in rows of desks, one teacher, one teacher's desk, one chalkboard, and maybe just out of sight, an overhead projector and a small bookcase. It's the typical classroom. It may not look exactly like yours, but it's certainly not unfamiliar.

I was teaching social studies and doing a pretty good job of it, if I do say so myself. The administration liked me; my colleagues liked me; my students liked me. Even the kids I failed enjoyed taking my courses over and over again. I worked hard, learning the material, devising fascinating lessons (and some not-so fascinating lessons), advising clubs, and meeting the students. Every evening I seemed to have a stack of papers to grade, a list of parents to call, another chapter to master. You get the picture. I was an underpaid teacher who loved what he was doing.

Then it happened: the second computer revolution in education. I'd missed the first one, which occurred in the 1960s. In that one, a bunch of computer terminals were linked together in a special room in the school and run by a large mainframe system that was housed in a neighboring state. The terminals acted as teaching machines, and students logged in

My life as a teacher.

The Computer Revolution #1

My Path to the One Computer Classroom

The Computer Revolution #2 (the latest one)

I felt as if I had moved into adjective heaven...everything was going to be wonderful.

and logged off for doses of learning. (Don't be surprised if this old revolution sounds very much like the new one.) That first effort didn't really catch on. The machines were too expensive and finicky, among other things.

The second computer revolution — the one I had walked in on — began in the late 70s and early 80s, or, then again, maybe the first one had never ended. In any case, the advent of the microcomputer sparked this second coming of interactive technology. Liberated from the long-reaching tentacles of the big system, computers became independent, accessible to anyone who wanted one. The machines' rapid spread into homes and into business and industry, especially, fueled the sense of urgency to bring them into the schools. Our children had to be prepared for the future. It wasn't just that students could be taught by computers. The kids also needed to learn about and be exposed to a technology that was quickly coming to dominate our society. (For many of you these sentences can be rewritten in the present tense and still apply.)

It was in the midst of all this excitement that the head of my department began handing me reprints from magazines. The computer, they said, was soon going to change my life. The stories they told astounded me. You know, like the one about the ten year old child who'd never written or spoken a word, but after just two hours with Logo had completed the sequel to War and Peace. I felt as if I had moved into adjective heaven — "powerful," "charming," and "interactive." Everything was going to be wonderful. I was still carrying out my daily duties, the mundane tasks of classroom management and the satisfying moments of

The Unfulfilled Promise of Computers

EXCITING

POWERFUL   **The Two Sides of Teaching**   CHARMING

The Management   The Craft

Guaranteed to fill all your teaching needs!!

ENGAGING   INTERACTIVE

enlightening a mind, but the future, the articles promised, was going to be even better. The computer would relieve the drudgery from *my* life. No more teacher as secretary, just teacher as teacher. It didn't sound too bad.

And who would lead us into this new world? The department head put his arm around my shoulder. I was the young one on the staff. What choice did I have? Besides, at the time, I was sharing a house with an economist who owned a personal computer. Now, I had never touched it, but the machine lived in my house. By proximity I had more computer experience than anyone else in the social studies department. I couldn't disagree.

We had an in-service workshop. The lights in the library were turned low and a man in a suit pushed a cart carrying a TRS 80 Model III computer into the room. We were hushed with anticipation. He showed us what at the time he called the cutting edge in social studies software, maybe even in *all* educational software: a program entitled *States and Capitals*. You may be familiar with it. An outline of a state appears on the screen, and the student has to type in the name of the capital before the timer runs out, or else New Jersey blows up.

I watched and I was amazed. You have to understand that I really knew nothing about computers at the time. I had watched my housemate sit for hours in a darkened room with the glare of the computer screen reflecting off of his ever-thickening glasses, but that was about it. I thought this *States & Capitals* program was great. After all, I was teaching a unit on U.S. geography, and I needed help. Believe it or not, many of my kids were just not that interested in states and capitals. Jefferson City, MO did not turn them on. They were, however, turned on by blowing up things, so I figured I had found a perfect match. They could blow up New Jersey, save humankind, and learn their geography.

I started to plan. The school had some computers, but none where I lived. The ones in the resource room, for special needs and remediation, remained off-limits. The math department, however, had about five or six of those Radio Shacks in a little computer lab. Maybe I could send some of my kids there. I pictured myself writing a pass to the lab for some of my

The computer promised to relieve the drudgery from my life.

A computer in-service

I was amazed.

The school had some computers, but none where I lived.

My Path to the One Computer Classroom

Maybe I could send my kids to the lab...

students who needed the extra work (the ones who kept returning to take my courses again and again.) You know the kind of kids I mean. In some schools they're called under-achievers, but teachers have many names for them — at-risk, lazy, slow, unmotivated. Some of the names I've heard are not particularly polite, nor do they show much respect for these kids who rarely find success in school. I'm sure that you can identify the group of students so labeled in your own school.

So I picture myself handing them the pass I've written, and they walk out the door. The computer lab is to the right, but I imagine them turning left toward the cafeteria or the parking lot. I couldn't trust these kids to seek out independent learning opportunities, even if it did include blowing up the states of our nation. If I wanted them to reach the desired destination and discover how much fun exploding states and capitals could be, I'd have to lead them there. But if I did that, the rest of my class would be left *unsupervised*. The computer "solution" wasn't relieving the drudgery, it was creating more management problems.

What's wrong with this picture?

I returned to the articles and promises I had been handed. Maybe I had misread them. Maybe the computer revolution was something different than I had imagined. The new picture I conjured resembled this illustration, and it reflected an advertisement run by Apple Computer: a computer on every desk for every child. It's still your classroom — desks in rows, you in front — but now each student has his or her own computer running a different program for each child. The Apple ad showed only seven kids in the classroom (I figured it was just camera angle, twenty other kids were hiding in

just camera angle, twenty other kids were hiding in the room somewhere), but otherwise it was almost identical to my depiction.

Tom Snyder says the ad reminds him of Highlights Magazine. Remember that August academic journal? I used to read it in the doctor's office when I was a young child. Every issue included a game called "What's wrong with this picture?" and you'd see a woman with a toothbrush in her hair. Let's play that game with my illustration. What's wrong with my picture? One "mistake," which also appeared in the Apple ad, should be obvious to anyone who's worked with technology in the classroom. Do you see any wires or cords? None of the computers are plugged in. How often is a roomful of computers this neat? In fact, how often is a roomful of computers arranged just like your classroom? Unless the space has been rebuilt and re-wired for technological integration, the decision-making on computer placement is generally more practical than pedagogical. Where do the machines go? They go where the plugs are. It's just another example of sound educational planning in the information age. And what about desk space? With the computer occupying most of the students' available writing area, how do they use paper and pencil? Or do those tools become obsolete in the computer revolution?

I'm certain that you can find more things wrong with this picture, but one final confusion stands out for its subtle, yet powerful, assumptions. What is the teacher in the picture doing? Each student is working on a different program, engrossed in an exciting, interactive piece of software. To whom is the teacher talking? Why is she even there? Is the teacher's role merely technical manager of instruction?

I found this vision of computers in education incredibly unappealing, even frightening. You have to consider our motivations as teachers. How many of you became teachers for the money? I certainly didn't. I remember, after three years of teaching, walking into the administration office and asking for a raise so that I'd have two digits before the comma in my salary. Cash flow isn't what made or makes teaching worthwhile. It's the relationship with the students, the magical moments of opening children's eyes to the world. The notion of managing

There must have been another 20 kids hiding somewhere.

How often is a room full of computers this neat?

The machines go where the plugs are...sound educational planning.

Teacher as technical manager of instruction

How many of you became teachers for the money?

My Path to the One Computer Classroom

The computer threatened to rob me of that one element that drew me to teaching.

While one student played with the computer, the rest of the class wondered why they weren't.

element that drew me to teaching. I rejected it, not only as unrealistic, but as unwanted, and I sought yet another alternative.

If I couldn't easily move my students out of my classroom to the computers (taking a group of students to the computer lab creates as much scheduling havoc as taking them to the library, or to any other shared resource in the school), nor could I anticipate my classroom soon becoming a computer lab, then I had to look for a compromise. I figured I would make a deal with the folks in the Math Department. I'd put one of their computers on a cart and wheel it into my classroom whenever I wanted some of my students to blow up New Jersey. This plan seemed simple enough, and it was not without precedent. I had always wheeled film and filmstrip projectors into my classroom when I needed them. This time the machine would be a computer, and it would occupy the same spot in the back of the classroom (near the plug) usually reserved for these more familiar pieces of educational technology.

But again a problem arose. Unlike film or filmstrips, which were for the whole class at once, the computer, I thought, was for only one or two students at a time. This illustration displays my predicament. While one student sat in the corner blowing up states and capitals, the rest of the class was doing something else, like wondering why they weren't in the corner blowing up states and capitals. The presence of the computer had created another management problem. How could I make sure that no student got left out of any important activity? I found myself rearranging the way I taught, creating ways to ro-

ways to rotate students through the computer game, so that I could use the technology to teach states and capitals. And changing my teaching style to accommodate a dinky piece of drill and practice software wasn't worth it.

Far from making my life easier, each vision of the computer appeared to make my life more difficult. The more I thought about it, the angrier I got. The technology had been introduced with such hope and promise, but I couldn't see what the machine was doing for me. I set off on a mission: to stop the flow of computers into schools. The technology became my enemy. Instead of spending money on machines, I argued, why not increase teacher salaries? I knew that such a resource redistribution would make me happier, more productive, and more equitably paid.

I took a leave of absence from teaching to enter a doctoral program at Harvard. There I sought ammunition for my battle from a familiar storehouse — history. I listened to what I had often told my history students when they asked the inevitable "Why are we learning this?" question. We study the past so that we can better understand the present and direct the future. We can learn from the experiences of others. So what insights can we gain from the efforts to bring previous "revolutionary" technologies into the classroom? A lot.

As I explored the past, the closeness of parallels to the computer revolution amazed me. I felt that we had been through this all before. One device after another has attempted to infiltrate the schools with great promise and fanfare only to fall far short of expectations. Let me illustrate this point with a little game. I'll present a quote about a revolutionary educational technology. You guess the year and the device being discussed. We'll start with an easy one:

"...much if not all the knowledge schools presently try to teach with such pain and expense and such limited success will be learned, as the child learns to talk, painlessly, successfully, and without organized instruction."

I found myself rearranging the way I taught so that I could use the technology.

Instead of spending money on machines, why not increase teacher salaries?

My war against computers

Name that Technology

Hint: Rt 90
        Fd 100

My Path to the One Computer Classroom

Have we been through all this before?

This foretelling of the near future comes from Seymour Papert's *Mindstorms* (1980). The computer, he claimed, can make schools obsolete with painless, natural learning. Is it true? Should we believe this bit of educational fortune-telling? Computer technology is not the first to foster predictions of the demise of formal schooling, and it likely won't be the last. We've heard these kinds of incredible claims before. Throughout history reports of the death of the classroom, however, have been somewhat exaggerated. From what year is this quote?

Does this sound familiar?

"...the existing system is utterly inefficient. The teacher...may pour it in the ear, or extract it from the printed page,...but unless he teaches through the eye...no satisfactory instruction can be conveyed."

You've probably heard this lament before. The problem with schools is too much talk, too many words. We need more visual learning. That was the call from Sir David Brewster in 1856 as he advocated the stereoscope and the magic lantern (precursors to the overhead projector). Using large slides and a flame, these machines could display large pictures on a blank wall, which generated great excitement among educational reformers. The old scientific adage, "seeing is believing," became a popular phrase supporting the introduction of slide shows into the schools. In 1893 it was proclaimed, "The age of illustration is upon us and illustrate we must if we hope to gain and hold the attention of young and old." (The call for schools to use the latest devices in order to compete for kids' attention with popular pastimes is a common tactic among technological reformers in education.) So the machines appeared, but not the revolution. Teachers encountered problems in the classroom. They had to turn out the lights to show the pictures, and you know what happens when you flick off the lights. A turn of the century article admitted that "/The first difficulty is that the room will be dark and tempt mischievous pupils to disorder." In addition, according to this author, students will use the lack of light as a reason for not doing their work. He anticipated an excuse no doubt familiar to most teachers who have employed a variety of visual aids in the classroom. He quoted the

The machines appeared, but not the revolution.

recalcitrant student in advance: "the room was so dark I could not see to write." Such difficulties, however, could be overcome. Just have each student, they suggested, bring in his or her own candle for personal lighting. That addition might eliminate the excuses, but it would also create a whopping fire hazard. Improvements in the technology led to its increased acceptance, but the predicted revolution in student learning never followed.

Darkness will "tempt mischievous pupils to disorder."

How about this prognostication?

"[It] is going to make school so attractive that a big army with swords and guns couldn't keep boys and girls out of it."

We had guns in my school, too.

The magic lantern offered still pictures, but they were so static. Children of the modern age needed more to hold their attention. As Thomas Edison, the author of the above quote (1911), watched kids entranced by his popular invention, he surmised the answer. Mix moving pictures with education and you'll have something that makes kids "want to go to school. You'll have to lick 'em to keep 'em away." Reformers heaped profound expectations upon the educational film industry. Movies were as good as good teachers and probably better than bad ones. They would teach everything from mathematics to morality, eliminate war, and rid the world of prejudice. Movie houses would replace school houses (the demise of the classroom again). Film projectors made their way into the schools, and you know what happened. (We had guards at my high school, but they had nothing to do with showing films in the classroom.) Familiar problems arose. You had to turn off those lights, which created the inevitable discipline troubles. The machines were complicated. I remember being on the AV team in junior high myself. I'd get out of class to load and run films for teachers too intimidated by the technology. I wasn't afraid to stick my finger in the loop to keep the movie from jumping. And the "software," the films themselves, were generally of very low quality. (Complicated hardware and bad software — is this starting to sound familiar?) Once again the anticipated

You know how kids love movies...

My Path to the One Computer Classroom

revolution failed to occur.

Let's try another quote:

"We are living in times of accelerated change....[this technology] can help [boys and girls] to be intelligent about important events;...it can bring them the good things of life...."

"[it] will ultimately be used as a substitute for certain teacher instruction."

Popular movies may have been exciting, but educational film tended to be relatively tame, boring, and outdated. Broadcasting, in the form of radio (the subject of these quotes from the early 1940's) and later TV, offered to supply a missing element to these generations of educational technology: immediacy. These devices could bring today's world right into the classroom as it happened, with none of the production delays that tended to make movies outdated even before they were released. And television, especially, brought together the best traits of all its predecessors — pictures, motion, sound, immediacy, plus it was easy to operate. The money poured in to support the growth of these machines in the classroom. Schools in Harlem, New York, and Oakland, California, became models of successful radio education. Hagerstown, Maryland, showed the world that Educational TV could work. But model schools didn't mean much for the rest of us, and again the revolution failed (at least, so far it's failed). Why?

Before answering that question, let's look at one more technology.

"[These instruments are] not uncommon, but are but little resorted to by the teacher."

"The teacher knows almost as little how to use it as his pupils."

This technology will surprise you. Reformers extolled the value of this device. They put them in schools across the nation, but — believe it or not — teachers just didn't use them. The instructors, everyone assumed, didn't know how. What was

You know how kids love radio...

You know how kids love TV...

They're available in the schools, but teachers just won't use them.

this revolutionary piece of classroom equipment? ...the chalkboard! These quotes from 1840 and 1842 reflect the frustration many felt with teachers' refusal to integrate this important new device into their teaching. So the reformers wrote detailed manuals, outlining specific chalkboard lessons step-by-step. They introduced courses at normal schools and other training institutions on chalkboard usage. They prodded and encouraged. All this to get teachers to take advantage of what is now a standard classroom tool.

Teaching teachers to use the chalkboard.

So why did the chalkboard gain near universal acceptance while later technologies have remained on the periphery, at best, of mainstream educational use? (After all, how many of you are applauded by your colleagues for showing a film in your class on Friday. Isn't it more like, "Oh, taking the day off, I see.") Was it just a matter of training? I doubt it. A lot more training and money went into film and TV without similar results. Consider, instead, the nature of the school into which the chalkboard was introduced and the one into which it was accepted. The 1840 school consisted of one room and 100, 200, even 300 or more students ranging in age from 5 to 16. The one room school house still dominated the American scene. When does a teacher in that environment, with that range of student age and ability, teach everybody at once? The big display advantage offered by the chalkboard was welcomed by college teachers at the time, but it held little value for common school instructors. Slate, textbooks, paper and pencil, the whole recitation and monitorial systems — all tools for having kids work alone — were embraced, but not the chalkboard. For that to happen the schools had to change.

What made the chalkboard succeed while other technologies failed?

And they did. By mid-century demographic and economic shifts in the nation had begun to bring many more children into the already crowded school system of the United States. New buildings and new mechanisms were needed to manage these growing numbers of students. It didn't take long for communities to adopt a structure based on age gradation. Build school buildings with many rooms and group students together by age for easier management. Group instruction, for which the chalkboard was a natural, grew easily out of the development of graded (first, second, third, and so on) schools. The

Why schools change

Learning lessons from the past

If the technology gets in the teacher's way, the teacher won't use it.

Teacher and technology must work together.

chalkboard now fit; teachers found it useful in their new environment, and it grew to be a staple of classroom life.

We can learn some important lessons from all this. First, schools do change, but they don't necessarily rearrange themselves because of some new instructional technology thrust into them. The chalkboard benefited from, but did not cause, a restructuring of schooling in the 19th century. More important factors were at work. There are many good reasons — and much debate — about how and why we should reorganize our schools, but doing it so that we can accommodate the idiosyncrasies of a particular technology, be it chalkboard or Apple II, isn't one of them.

Second, if the technology doesn't support the classroom environment — if it creates a discipline problem or undermines teacher control, either of pedagogy or management — it won't be used. You determine what appears on the chalkboard, but how much control do you have over the flow of a film or the content of a spontaneous radio or TV broadcast? How well can you even plan to integrate these electronic devices into your teaching style? I can easily sit at home and devise a lesson that incorporates the chalkboard or even the overhead projector (a 1960's version of the magic lantern that is safer and allows you to leave the lights on). What I write on a piece of paper can be made to appear on either rather simply. Live broadcasts, on the other hand, are impossible to preview let alone plan around. And previewing a 90 minute film during a 42 minute preparation period remains a trick I have yet to master. (How many teachers own 16mm projectors at home?)

Teacher and technology must work in concert for mutual goals. Let me offer one final quote. What classroom application is being described here?

"[This device] appealed at once to the eye and to the ear, thus naturally forming the habit of attention, which is so difficult to form by the study of books.... Whenever a pupil does not fully understand, [it] will have the opportunity...of enlarging and making intelligible."

This description captures it all — sight, sound, and spontaneous interactivity, offering meaningful intervention with each student misstep. But this 1855 quote doesn't describe a computer. It's a union of powerful technology with the most versatile interface ever invented — a chalkboard in the hands of a teacher. That's the image, a tool for the professional teacher, a master craftsperson.

The most versatile interface ever invented

With all this in mind, I offer a final vision of the computer in the school. I first witnessed this application of the technology when, during year one of my great war against computers, I visited a 5th grade classroom in Cambridge, MA. I had been looking at schools using computers all around the area — Logo labs, library resource centers, and so on — and I was armed with a healthy amount of knee-jerk skepticism. This classroom, however, set itself far apart from the others I'd seen. The teacher was Tom Snyder. I'd heard about him from an old college roommate who had worked with Tom's new business partner (Tom had just started a small software company). My former roommate told me that Tom and I were similar kinds of teachers. I found that hard to believe. After all, Mr. Snyder was using computers in his classroom.

Tom Snyder's class was something different.

But what I saw changed my mind. The class was great. The kids were working in small groups, running energy companies and seeking more efficient sources of fuel. Each group of students was having a dynamic mini-discussion, and Tom was moving from group to group playing devil's advocate. It could have been one of my classes, except mine always seemed to have a higher level of chaos. Then I noticed something else different from my classrooms. There was a computer in the corner, and the groups of students were taking turns using it. The program, Energy Search, was one of several Tom had written (the *Search Series* was published by McGraw-Hill) to help him run the simulations he was already doing in his classroom. And it was helping him in the background, while keeping the student interactions at the forefront.

Groups of students were taking turns using the computer.

Maybe the computer did have a place in the classroom. But it didn't belong exclusively to the students. It belonged to the teacher, and the teacher is the one who should control and determine its use. The technology should serve educational goals, not direct them. That's what Tom Snyder was demon-

The computer in the teacher's hands

Don't stop! Keep reading!

strating, and that's the philosophy that's driven him and his associates, including myself, since the advent of this second computer revolution.

Let's Decide Where We're Going Before We Try to Get There.

Now that so many schools have invested so heavily in computer hardware and software, many teachers, computer coordinators, and administrators are feeling great pressure to begin or extend their use of the equipment. They are actively, and sometimes begrudgingly, seeking activities to do with their machines, preferably applications that show off the wonders of this new technology (programs that offer print outs are very popular). "Okay, we've got the computers," these educators begin, "What can we do with them?" Unfortunately, this type of searching and questioning can quickly lead you deep into the world of high-tech and out of the world of the classroom.

The computer, and all its attachments, can so easily amaze, astound, and dazzle. "Wow, look at all those colorful graphics!" "Listen to that sound." "Check out all that data." "Awesome." "Incredible." All of a sudden, you're in adjective heaven, blinded by science, struggling to find a way to use this fantastic device in your classroom. Use of the technology becomes an end in itself, leading, rather than being led by, you and your objectives. You begin to wonder how you can rearrange your life so that your kids can, to steal a phrase from Tom, "blow up adverbs with diphthong bombs." But technology is supposed to serve, not dictate, our needs.

This situation is not new. I remember when I was teaching ancient history, preparing to have the kids memorize the pharaohs in order. The list was so conveniently displayed in the textbook, and the activities at the end of the chapter included that suggestion: "Have your students memorize the pharaohs in order." It was so tempting and easy merely to follow the technology, in this case the textbook, and too many times I did. But we have to stop ourselves; get back to fundamentals, the bigger questions.

The wrong question

Blinded by science

Following the technology rather than leading it

Let's decide where we're going before we try to get there.

Understand the technology, then forget about it.

First, a couple of questions

Setting goals

"Do we have to do this?"

The best way to approach educational technology, new or old, computer or otherwise, is to first understand it, and then forget about it. It is valuable to recognize the new opportunities made available by new technologies, but these devices should not necessarily direct our efforts. Let me suggest two questions you need to address before you consider how to employ technology: 1. What do I want my students to be able to do? 2. What methods should I use to help them achieve those goals? Now I am not saying that you must commit yourself to lifetime answers to these inquiries, only that they must be discussed and then discussed again. And only after that exercise can you begin to figure out what tools, including the computer, will help you get you to where you want to be.

Where do I want to be?

Let's start with the first question. As anxious reformers push technology at schools and at you in particular, you must remember that the goal is not more teachers and students using computers. You would never, for instance, sit down to construct a lesson thinking, "Now what can I do that will use the chalkboard." On the contrary, you decide what you want to cover and then look for the tools and mechanisms that will best help you do that. Educational technologies are tools to be employed toward educational ends. But what are those ends? Whether you teach science or social studies, first grade or high school, you are attempting to move your students toward something larger that goes beyond your classroom and the semester final. But what is it? What are the goals of schooling anyway?

The question of the purpose of education is huge and may well be unresolvable (in fact, maybe it should be unresolvable). Nonetheless, it needs to be addressed and re-addressed because the answer directs our use or misuse of the tools for teaching and learning. One of the main problems with talking about "the big picture," however, is that it seems so far from the tasks at hand — what are you going to do in class tomorrow? — and it also seems out of your control. Maybe that's why we rarely do it, and why it is so tempting to simply focus on memorizing the pharaohs. We need to take time to ask ourselves some "why" questions. "Why do I teach this?" And

Let's decide where we're going before we try to get there.

"Why do my students need to know that?" (Your students certainly don't hesitate to ask these questions, whether you hear them or not.) But thinking about why we do what we do takes up a lot of valuable time and doesn't necessarily lead anywhere. We are often like our own students who get impatient with classroom discussions that have no right or wrong answers. "Why are we wasting time? Just tell us what we need to know for the test," they say. The immediate, practical concerns take precedence. So, even though some of you may want to skip ahead to the chapter on practical suggestions for your classroom, I urge you to invest a little time here.

No right answers

Ideally, at this point, I would ask you to make a list of your goals, a list of what you want your students to be able to do when they are done with school. Then we would talk about and more closely define the items on your list. Unfortunately, we can't do that. So instead, I'll share with you some of the most common responses I have received from teachers across the country of all disciplines and grade levels:

How do others answer this question?

I want my students to...
- have mastered basic skills
- be able to solve problems and make decisions
- be good citizens and intelligent voters
- have a sense of community
- be good critical thinkers
- be motivated to continue learning
- have life and social skills
- be productive

What would you add to this list?

Of course, each item on this list generates it own set of questions and its own sub-list. What, for instance, are the basic skills students need to master? What do problem-solving and critical thinking mean? Are life skills different for different students in different circumstances? And the items on the list make horrible behavioral objectives. How do you measure, for example, whether a student is "productive?" Must you wait until he or she finds gainful employment after graduation?

Behavioral objectives? Yuk!

Oddly enough, it is the ambiguities in the answers that make addressing this question so exciting and useful. Even though

Let's decide where we're going before we try to get there.

Try it with your colleagues.

Turning vision into reality

My favorite class...

The kids were using, not just remembering, what I'd taught them.

you and your colleagues may be able to reach an agreement on a general list like the one above, I bet that you will do battle over the details. It's a refreshing discussion. I urge you to give it a try, even if the ensuing argument occurs only with voices in your own head. Start with the list on the previous page if you want. What would you add? What do the items mean? Construct your own personal agenda for why you do what you do.

How do I get there?

Once you have a vision of where you want your students to end up, you should consider how to get them there. What methods do and should you employ to develop critical thinking skills, ensure the acquisition of fundamental information, encourage wise decision-making, and so on? Start with what you do now, with familiar successful lessons that work.

I remember my best class; it still makes me smile. In fact, it gets better with age. I was teaching history, and as the kids walked into the classroom, one student asked me if I'd seen the recent news about violence in the Middle East. (I always thought it a sign of success that my students took an active interest in the world around them.) I prompted an elaboration and the next thing I knew, a discussion had erupted. "I can't believe we let those terrorists attack us." "Yeah, how can we let Khadafy run Iran?" I correct them, "Khadafy is in Libya; the Ayatollah is in Iran." "We should attack them or something." "We can't do anything." "Sure we can. We can do like Teddy Roosevelt did in Central America?"

WHOA! Teddy Roosevelt? I taught about that months ago. I was starting to enjoy this, but it only got better.

"We can't interfere. The nation is like it was under Wilson — isolationist. The people don't want to get involved." And on it went.

The kids kept going, and I was loving it. I listened. I arbitrated. I corrected. I offered an occasional prompt or question. Then the bell rang, but they didn't move, didn't jump up to meet their friends in the hall between classes! They weren't finished talking. I had to urge them out the door, and as they left they were still going at it. It felt so good, but it still wasn't over. It's lunchtime and I'm in the cafeteria doing one

Let's decide where we're going before we try to get there.

of the great things teachers get to do, making sure the kids throw away their garbage, and I spot some of my students. They're sitting together talking, arguing, debating. I'm feeling great. Then the next morning I get a call from a parent. At first I'm nervous — did she find out her kid hasn't memorized the pharaohs? But it's a good call. She says, "Something strange happened last night. My son had dinner with us." By itself a major accomplishment, but there was more. "He came home, read the newspaper, watched the news on TV and wanted to talk about what was going on in the world. He mentioned something about what happened in class..."

And they carried the discussion home with them.

What more could I ask for? My students were remembering and *using* what I had taught them. They were actively curious and concerned about issues and events. And they were carrying what they had learned with them not just outside of my classroom, but outside of the school building. It was dynamic, exciting, and fun for my students *and* for me. I wanted to have those feelings everyday, every class. Unfortunately, they occurred all too rarely.

It feels great!

Now take a moment to recall or imagine your own best lesson as a teacher, your favorite class as a student. Relive those magic moments that make teaching worthwhile. Remember how good and satisfying it feels when everything clicks together. What memories are stirred in you? An incredible class discussion? Some dynamic small group activity? A classroom simulation perhaps? Maybe even a stirring lecture? It doesn't matter. Great teaching and wonderful classroom experiences come in many forms. What methodologies would you add to this list?

What are your best classes?

Here's what I do in the classroom:
- Discussion
- Cooperative learning
- Independent research
- Lecture and Demonstration
- Simulation
- Role playing
- Games
- Drill

29

Let's decide where we're going before we try to get there.

Matching goals and strategies

Add the computer to your arsenal.

Ideally, you are constantly matching a selection from your goals list with one or more of these approaches all within a particular content area. For example, you might use a combination of drill, games, and cooperative learning to encourage student mastery of some basic skills, like the multiplication tables, while simultaneously developing social skills. On the other hand, you might choose to employ a role-playing simulation for fostering citizenship and decision-making while exploring the events of the Revolutionary War.

On the surface, it all seems rather simple. You pick a goal and then, based on that goal and the characteristics of the student group, select a strategy from a broad repertoire of methodologies that will enable you to accomplish that goal. Then, finally, you choose the tools necessary to carry out your plan. You should view the computer (along with the appropriate software) as one of those tools, a weapon in your arsenal of devices (an arsenal that includes everything from chalkboards and textbooks to board games and film projectors) that you can employ with your students to achieve your own visions.

Much of the rest of this book, in fact, is devoted to describing how one single computer from your arsenal can be a powerful classroom tool, how it can help you organize and lead lectures and discussions, assist you in managing small cooperative learning groups, and even relieve some of the administrative burdens that infringe upon preparation time and teaching. But before launching into those descriptions, we need to address one final issue: access.

Getting Computers into Teachers' Hands

Access is essential.

Let's talk about that arsenal for one more moment. As teachers we use some weapons more than others. Part of that usage difference is explained by personal preference, part by the quality of the particular tool. But one obstacle that can severely limit employment (maybe deployment is a better term here) falls into a different realm: lack of access. All the hype about how the computer can transform your classroom means nothing if you don't have the opportunity to integrate the machine into your way of life. You've got to have access and proof that the device can be valuable. Think again about the film

Let's decide where we're going before we try to get there.

projector. How often do we use it, and how often do we just show movies?

Let me explain. At one point when I was teaching, I floated; I didn't have a classroom of my own. Each period I was in somebody else's room. I really didn't mind because I didn't want the responsibility of decorating my classroom walls. I'm color blind; I have enough trouble getting my clothes to match. In any case, my work space was a desk in the social studies office, a small room with four desks, a wall of bookcases, a ditto machine, a phone for incoming calls only (they didn't trust us not to call overseas to enhance the world cultures curriculum), and another desk that served as the foreign language department office. I also had a broken two-drawer filing cabinet. It wasn't broken when I started. It had one of those push-in locks, but no key. Within a week someone had pushed in the lock, so I had to break it open. Then it was broken. In addition, I occasionally shared my desk with in-house suspension (you know, when they kick someone out of school but refuse to reward him by letting him leave).

Within these circumstances, if I wanted to preview a film, I had double trouble: space and time. I had to sign up to get a projector during a free 42-minute preparation period during the week, and then I had to find space in that little office to watch the 64-minute film. I didn't have a projector at home; I had to do it at school. So I'd wheel a manual threader (all the automatic threading projectors were always checked out) into the office, seek out a small piece of blank wall — maybe 5" x 5" — and turn on the movie. Of course, I had to leave the lights on so as not to disturb the suspended kid sitting at my desk rifling through my papers. If the film didn't break in the first five minutes, it got my stamp of approval and I'd show it in class the next day.

I may be exaggerating a bit, but the first time I viewed many films all the way through was in class. I just didn't have time or access elsewhere. After I'd seen a movie a few times, I had developed some ideas about how to really use it, but often, I just showed it. Software use may not be much different. If the only available computers are in the computer lab, and you have to fight with the students to get at them, your use of any software

The school as teacher's office

How do you preview a film?

Where do you really do your work?

Let's decide where we're going before we try to get there.

My office was my dining room table.

is bound to be limited. Even if the computer is in your classroom, that doesn't guarantee access. My real work space, whether I had a classroom or roamed as a floater, was my dining room table at home. A few teachers stayed late after school to work in their classrooms, but many seemed to race the kids out the door when the final bell rang. I myself found it difficult to get privacy anywhere in the school building. I was always surrounded by students, and I just couldn't turn them away. So I took my work home.

I may appear to have strayed from my topic somewhat here, but we can't ignore the realities of school and teacher life when talking about technology. If computers don't support teachers where they work and the way they work, teachers are not going to find ways the machines can assist them in the classroom. This issue has been addressed directly by some schools in the country.

In 1987, a school district in the State of Washington (Lake Washington district, in fact) sought to encourage its teachers to explore how the computer could help enhance their teaching. The district's approach is worth noting. They held a voluntary in-service over the summer concerning computer applications — word processing, data base management, etc. They offered teachers who attended these workshops an interesting form of pay — an Apple IIGS computer for home use. In fact, they specifically told the teachers not to bring the machines into the schools. The folks in Lake Washington were smart. They knew that access was the key. Let the teachers discover for themselves how the computer could help them where they live, even develop a dependency on the machine, and then they themselves might find a way to bring it into the classroom.

It was a great idea. The following year, the teachers asked

Elements of Successful Classroom Technology

- **Support of Teacher Control**
  Use of the technology must <u>not</u> make the teacher's management task <u>more</u> difficult.

- **Pedagogic Flexibility**
  The technology must support the various ways teachers teach.

- **Accessibility**
  Teachers must have access to it where they work, both inside and outside of the classroom.

Computers for teachers!

Let's decide where we're going before we try to get there.

for modems. They wanted to start sharing ideas, lesson plans, activities. Many can no longer imagine how they ever wrote without a word processor. I myself can't believe that anyone ever finished a doctoral thesis before the invention of writing utilities. It's a dependency, but not a bad one. I'm sure a number of you are already hooked. And even if the computer never makes it into the classroom, it will have had a positive impact on the classroom indirectly. It has helped rejuvenate and excite some teachers. It has made them more productive on the administrative side of their lives.

Get yourself hooked.

Unfortunately, Lake Washington is unusual. Teachers are not always figured into the equation that determines distribution of resources. In 1988, for instance, the Office of Technology Assessment of the Congress of the United States studied the use of computers in schools. In their report, "Power On! New Tools for Teaching and Learning," they counted an average of one computer for every thirty students. It's interesting to note that they didn't compile a teacher-to-computer ratio. The numbers would have been much closer to one-to-one.

How about figuring teacher-to-computer ratios, too?

It doesn't make sense. When textbooks began making their way into the classrooms of the early 19th century, the teacher was among the first to receive one. We wouldn't expect successful student use otherwise. Why should we overlook the teacher in the distribution of computers?

Imagine giving a textbook to every student but none to the teacher.

Fortunately, the call for greater teacher access gets louder every year. As part of its school restructuring efforts, the American Federation of Teachers pushes for making computers available to classroom practitioners. The National Education Association has called for a computer on every teacher's desk by the early 1990s. IBM presents a school network plan that connects classroom teachers to curricular and management software along with access to centralized information. And just about everyone in the Teacher Empowerment movement supports the computer as a tool for professionalizing teaching.

Support from reform movements

If there is to be a computer revolution in education, it won't start inside the classroom, but outside of it. That's where many computer-using teachers started. In fact, that's actually where I started. That housemate of mine who owned a Radio Shack Model III wrote a grading program for me to use at home, where

Let's decide where we're going before we try to get there.

I started with a grading program.

Messing with the fudge factor

My kids stopped challenging their grades.

I usually did my grades. The program was simple, straightforward and did exactly what I wanted it to do. And it made my life easier. I don't know about you, but I usually knew what final grade I was going to give a kid before I averaged his scores. I'd look at him or her and say B-, maybe C+. Then I'd sit down with my gradebook and calculator and plug in tests, homework, projects, papers, and then "in-class participation" — my fudge number. The results usually matched my predictions, but there were always borderline cases. That's when I'd play with the in-class number until it came out the way I wanted. Don't get me wrong. I was fair. The kids always knew where they stood. In some ways I was just gearing up for the battle I knew would follow.

When I finally gave the students their grades, I'd call them up to my desk, one by one, show them the numbers, their letter grade, and then wait for the argument. I got one maybe 30 to 50% of the time. "But Mr. Dockterman, I did all that homework, didn't I?" "I should have gotten a higher grade on my project." "Can I take that last test over again?" Sometimes a student would be right. He or she did deserve a higher grade. And I was usually ready to give it, after they begged for it. But seriously, grades are so subjective, you need a fudge factor. The grading program made it easier for me to fudge the numbers and to track each student more closely. I had to do the same amount of data input I did before with a calculator, but with the computer the numbers didn't disappear when I was finished. I could continue to play with them.

There was a downside, in an ironic sort of way, of computer processed grading. When I showed kids their grades, instead of displaying a handwritten sheet of paper, I offered them a computer printout. They no longer argued. All of a sudden, because the numbers were being generated by a computer, my students stopped challenging their grades. (Other teachers have told me of similar experiences.) In a way, that was good, but I had always depended on them to keep me honest. I had to explain that I was still the subjective author of their evaluations. You know, if we teach our kids anything about computers, it should be to maintain a healthy amount of skepticism about whatever the machines tell us.

It takes time (and access), but whether you begin with

Let's decide where we're going before we try to get there.

grading programs or word processors, once you discover one way the computer can make your life simpler (although it may appear more complicated at first), a host of other possibilities will appear. The key, though, is starting with what you already do. That was Apple's marketing approach to business. I loved those ads — a picture of an executive-type person with the following quote under his face: "I want a computer that makes me better at what I do. And I don't do computers." As teachers we want devices that help us improve our craft, directly or indirectly. If the computer can ease the administrative tasks we perform, then it will free us to devote more energy to the classroom, whether or not the machine itself ever finds its way there. And that's good enough.

Start with what you already do.

Of course, despite this demand for true access, in many schools the computer remains out of easy reach for many classroom teachers. Maybe the computers are tied up in labs or wheeled around on carts. You still have options. Take a machine home on weekends or over the summer. You can even try something simple in the classroom, not a complex data base manager, but a straightforward push-button application.

Isn't it enough for the computer to make our lives a little bit easier?

A number of possibilities are described in the next chapters. You will find specific ideas for how the computer can help you both inside and outside of your classroom walls.

A Tool for The Professional Teacher

I'm going to ask you to make one more list, but I promise that it will be easy. List the most significant problems you face as a teacher. Here is a sample of the typical response. What else would you add?

- Lack of time
- Too few resources
- Discipline
- Lack of support from home
- Not enough money or respect
- Administrative busy work
- Insufficient training
- Class size
- Apathy and burn-out

What's the problem?

This litany of difficulties can be a bit depressing, and hopefully you suffer from as few of them as possible.

Now, I'm not going to suggest that the computer can make these problems go away. It can't make your classes smaller or your day longer. It is naive to think that the purchase of any technology will automatically resolve complicated issues of time, resources, and behavior. But I will argue that access to the computer and the appropriate software can help, and help significantly. After some initial investment, you may find that the use of the computer actually saves you time and helps you better manage your students.

The computer won't solve all your problems...

The picture on the following page lists some general ways a good teacher can take advantage of a single computer both as an administrative tool and as an instructional aide. In the next four chapters I will offer some specific examples of products, lessons, and activities that you can use both inside and outside of your classroom. Some of the suggestions, a

...but it can help.

A Tool for the Professional Teacher

What Can a Good Teacher do with a Computer?

Manage responsibilities and paperwork

Make dazzling presentations

Lead incredible discussions

Manage dynamic cooperative learning activities

Inspire enlightening self-discovery

number of which I have gathered from talking to teachers across the country, you will be able to implement directly, others might spark some original ideas of your own. In any case, keep in mind your unique situation, your resources, time and financial constraints, priorities, and educational philosophy.

Also keep in mind the way you want your life as a teacher to be. How do you see yourself? Your occupation? Your mission? The following pages focus specifically on a number of applications that should be a standard part of any set of teacher tools. Underlying the programs described, though, is something more — an image of teacher professionalism that is reflected as much by attitude and desire as it is by any set of instructional devices. A tool is ultimately only as good as the user. It can take you only as far as you are willing to go. You have an opportunity here to use the computer as part of a larger effort to improve your status and position in the educational realm. Just as the computer has enhanced the abilities of professionals in the business world, so too can the technology be a part of efforts to increase teacher empowerment and professionalism. Through the detail that follows, never lose sight of the bigger picture.

Any tool is only as good as its user.

Electronic Gradebook

In the last chapter, I mentioned that my introduction to computers in school came through my gradebook. That's not necessarily the best path for everyone. Nor do you need to have a program written specifically for you as I did. A number of grading programs are currently on the market that are simpler and more powerful than the one my nerdy (I'm only kidding)

A Tool for the Professional Teacher

housemate created for me.

My favorite commercial grading/attendance utility, the one I've been able to use without ever opening the documentation, is called *Grade Busters 1/2/3*. The on-screen directions walk you through setting up each class, and if you keep your records up-to-date (a stumbling block for a number of teachers), you'll reap worthwhile results. How often, for instance, have you wanted to know where a number of your students stood in the middle of a grading period but hesitated to find out because you were overwhelmed at the prospect of averaging grades more than once? How often have you kicked yourself for not

GradeBusters 1/2/3

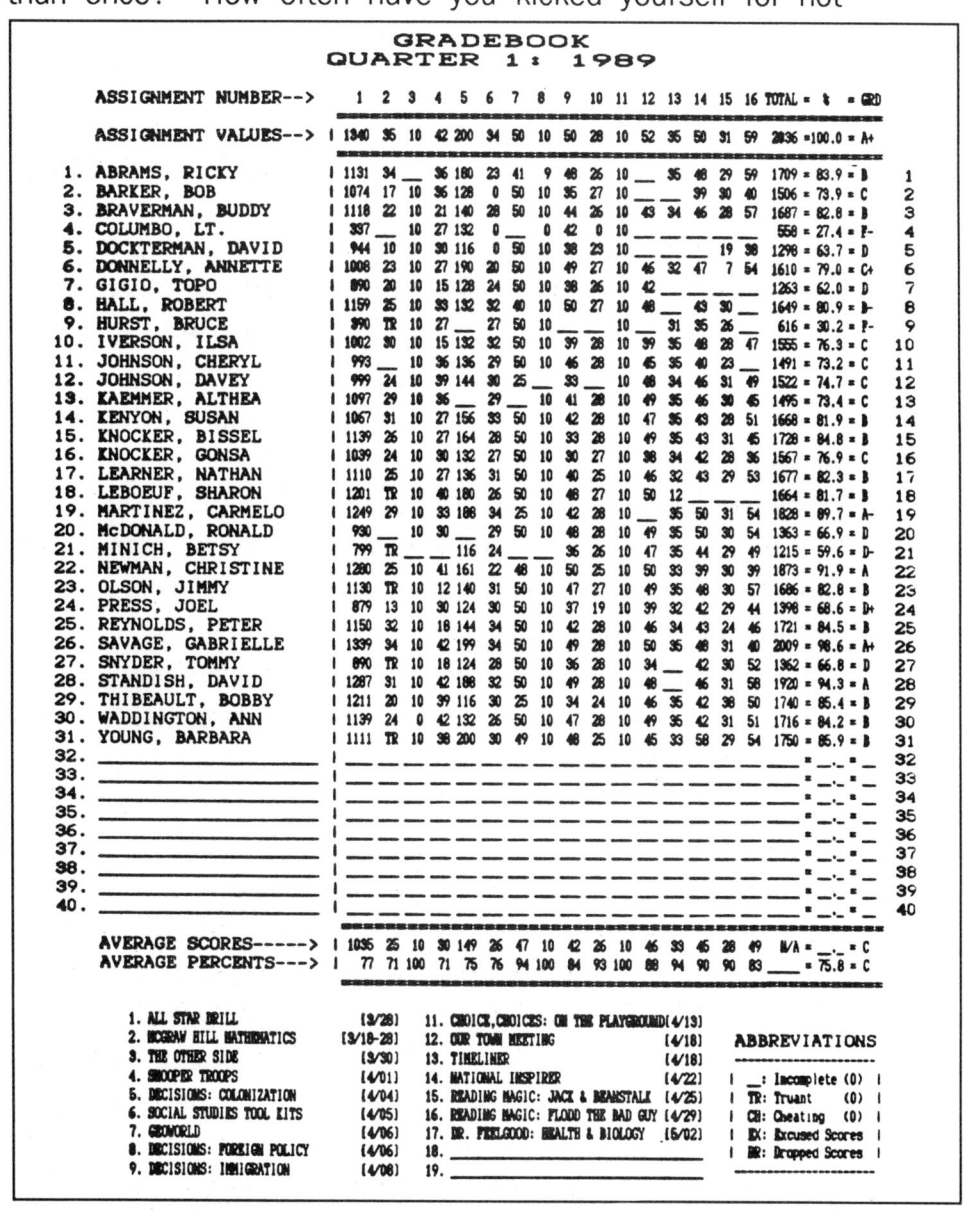

39

A Tool for the Professional Teacher

Have you ever been frustrated by your gradebook?

The ripple effects can be seen in student performance.

"actually the program has allowed me to spend more of my time teaching."

recognizing before the end of the semester how one of the quiet students in a class had gradually stopped doing any work? How often have you had to re-average a student's grade because the result just didn't seem right? How often have you given a test or assignment that was too hard (or too easy) and struggled to figure out what to do with the abnormal grade? Or how often have you cursed at your hard-copy gradebook for being too small, too hard to change (don't you hate it when students are added or subtracted from your roster), or too flimsy?

With a program like *Grade Busters 1/2/3* you eliminate all of these difficulties. You can get printouts, averages, distributions, specific records on any student or class anytime you want. If the data has been typed in (you have to record it somewhere, sometime), you can perform all these functions with the mere press of a button. This sample printout illustrates the kind of information available to you. Play around with it for a while. You'll discover options that make what you already do easier and what you never thought you could do possible.

And the ripple effects may surprise you. I've heard a number of testimonials from teachers who've found that gradebook programs indirectly actually help to improve student performance. By making it easier to let students know when their grades are dipping or assignments are missing, you can spark your pupils into action. One teacher from New Jersey, Dana Freeman, had this to say about a piece of grading software he had discovered.

The most important result of using this program is that my students appear to be taking a more active and responsible role in their own education. Oh, as soon as I begin to detect a pattern, I pull the student aside with the strong suggestion that the situation be corrected <u>soon</u> — before I have to contact the home. But, more and more...I find that students are having to be talked to less and less about those missing assignments. Does this mean that I'm seeking to shun some of my duties? No, actually the program has allowed me to spend more of my time — TEACHING!

That sounds like a worthwhile effort to me.

A Tool for the Professional Teacher

Information Management

How old are your dittoes? Do they look like blue jeans that have been washed too many times — sort of a faded out blue and white? I'll never forget sitting at a typewriter (not a keyboard, but a typewriter) typing out end-of-semester tests on a pile of dittoes for each of my classes. I can't even count the number of times I got halfway through a page before realizing that I'd forgotten to remove the little tissue page that separates the blue ink from the white master, and I'd have to start all over again. It was frustrating. I was always incredibly careful with each keystroke because mistakes were so hard to correct. Once completed each ditto became a treasured masterpiece. Of course, those tests didn't necessarily apply to a particular class year in and year out. And every year I dreaded the prospect of changing them, because I couldn't *change* them. I had to redo them from scratch.

Then we got photocopiers, or at least we got one in the central office building. (They even threatened, at one point, to take away our ditto machines.) This new device was supposed to solve the problem of old, unreadable dittoes. All we had to do was submit nice typewritten pages a week ahead of time, and we'd get back a stack of highly legible reproductions. Of course, I never understood how we were supposed to do, say, pop quizzes, if we had to have created them a week ahead of time. In any case, the photocopier only relieved my problem slightly. It was easier to type on a blank piece of paper than a ditto master, but it still wasn't really any easier to change or edit.

Computers, on the other hand, make it very easy to edit. You create a test one year, change the information on the disk the next year, print it out (you can even make dittoes), and you've got a new master copy. You can do worksheets, project assignments, you name it. At the simplest level, all you need is a good word processor. Some packages, however, like the *Exam-in-a-Can* mathematics series, actually create unique tests complete with graphs and tables based on the specific objectives you indicate. You can also buy dedicated test or worksheet generators that have built-in question formats, but such features can be constraining.

I used to treasure my dittoes.

Then came the photocopiers.

How do you get a "pop" quiz photocopied a week ahead of time?

Let the computer, not the paper, manage your information.

41

A Tool for the Professional Teacher

The key, regardless of the software you use, is to let the computer rather than sheets of paper manage your information. The computer allows you to build upon what you have already done much more easily than a traditional file folder or lesson plan book can. You never have to re-invent the wheel. It's saved on disk, waiting for you to rearrange it, move it around, even reconstruct it.

My contact with parents needed improvement.

Letters to Parents

If I had to highlight one aspect of my teaching I wished most to improve, it would have been contact with parents. I didn't do it enough, and I had lots of excuses. With prepping lessons, grading papers, advising clubs, and sleeping I just didn't have time. They were hard to reach. I was sometimes intimidated by the parents of my students. (I don't know why. Maybe it was general teacher insecurity.) The list goes on.

I called the homes of kids who struggled in class, who were in danger of failing. I tried to let parents of hard-working pupils know when their kids did something exceptional, but a large population in the middle was neglected. A simple word-processor and a printer would have allowed me, as they have enabled a number of teachers, to greatly increase and enhance the level of communication between school and parents.

It's easy. Write a form letter (see left) and just fill in different names. If you want to get fancy, you can even get a data base and filing program that

```
                                February 8, 1989
Parent name
street address
town, state   zip

Dear [parent name],

Just a short note to keep you updated about
what's going on in [student's name]'s history
class.  We're wrapping up the Egyptians next
week and will then tackle the ancient Greeks.

You should be seeing mummy wrappings or pyramid
blocks around the house.  We're in the midst of
a big final project for the unit.  I've been
assured that everyone in the class is hard at
work.  If you're not seeing the evidence of that
work, please give your child a prompt and me a
call.

I'll be dropping you a line again shortly as the
grading period comes to a close.  If, however,
you have questions or just wish to talk before
that time, simply call the school and leave a
message.  I'll get back to you.

                        Sincerely,

                        David Dockterman
```

A Tool for the Professional Teacher

will do that for you… and address the envelopes too. You only have to write the letter once; the computer will print it out over and over again. Without too much additional time, you can even customize each letter with specific comments about each student's performance. If you've got nothing to say, let the basic letter stand. Each print out is separate so the typeface is consistent throughout the letter, unlike the sweepstakes offers you receive in the mail.

Just write the letter once and change the names each time you print it out.

One teacher, Donald Bullock of California, has actually researched the effectiveness of this kind of letter writing effort. Comparing computer-assisted communication with traditional methods, Bullock found very positive results. Here's a summary (for a more detailed description see the *Proceedings of NECC '88*):

Positive results of study

> The teachers using computers reported a dramatic improvement in the effectiveness of their teacher-parent communication. Parents expressed an appreciation to the teachers for the effort they made in creating the letters. Teachers noticed that parents became more interested in what was happening at school. Most importantly the teachers noticed that they were able to reach thirty parents in the same time that they could reach only four using traditional methods.
>
> Parents responding to the survey were overwhelmingly in favor of the letters they received. Most parents perceived that the form letters were written specifically for them — not to the whole class. The survey results showed that parents felt that they received more information from the teachers when the teachers used the computers than they did when more traditional methods of communication were used.

The parents thought that the form letters were written specifically for them.

It's a great way for you to become a hero. The parents will love it. The administration will love it. And it won't be long before you begin to open a regular dialog with parents. When that happens you can explore possible ways to get them more involved in what's going on in your classroom. With just a small

Become a hero to parents and administration.

43

A Tool for the Professional Teacher

investment of time and energy, you can take a giant step toward improving the school/home connection. And you will be pleased with the spillover impact on student behavior.

Nifty Materials

In December 1987 Apple ran another ad that caught my eye (I wonder why IBM and Tandy ads don't leave me with such strong impressions?). This one appeared in *The Wall Street Journal*. Obviously, it was not meant for teachers. How many of you check your investments everyday? Nonetheless, Apple presented a message to businesspeople that also speaks very strongly to classroom instructors. The three-page spread opens with a large picture of a device familiar to the worlds of both education and industry: an overhead projector. In the upper right hand corner of the page is the following message: "WARNING: Improper operation of this machine may cause headaches, nausea and drowsiness."

I could identify with that image, and the inside text elaborated. Apple, the ad proclaimed, was here "to save humanity (and you) from the deadliest of sins: Boring people in public." No more "brain-numbing overheads, eye-glazing slides, and soul-deadening presentation handouts." Although the ad was describing a typical business meeting, my mind conjured up a vision of an all-too-typical classroom. As a student and as a teacher, I know that I had been both bored and boring. My students were none too shy about announcing, sometimes in rather unpleasant ways, when their attention had begun to drift from the lesson at hand. The promise that I could easily create "dazzling, scintillating, graphically compelling overheads, 35mm color slides, and leave-behinds that don't get left behind" was very compelling. It still is.

So, one other way the computer can be an asset *outside* of your classroom is by helping you create nifty materials for you to bring *into* your classroom. I now depend on my Macintosh computer and a LaserWriter printer to make overheads (not always dazzling, scintillating, and graphically compelling, but better than I could before) for presentations and in-service workshops I do across the country. And believe me, a group of

Another Apple ad

I've been both bored and boring in the classroom.

"leave-behinds that don't get left behind"

A Tool for the Professional Teacher

bored teachers is much more difficult to manage than a group of bored children. I'll welcome any device, as I did when I was teaching, that helps me enliven my classroom. We all do. We build incredible displays for our classroom walls and desks. I remember, on a visit to The Learning Exchange in Kansas City (a fantastic place, by the way), helping a teacher carry a giant laminated creation out to her car — something neat for her classroom. The computer can be a part of this kind of effort.

You can make great stuff for your classroom.

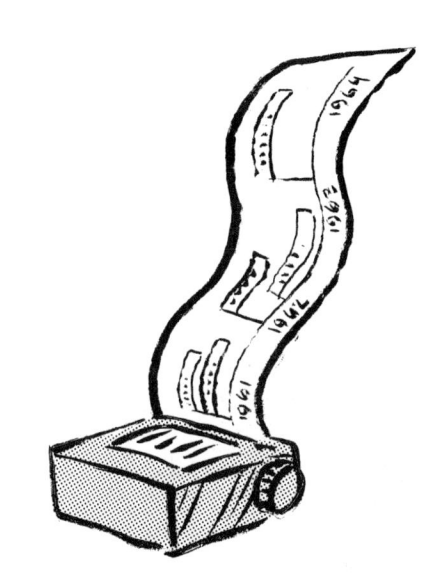

Of course, not all of you have access to the latest in high-tech equipment and presentation software. Not that teachers shouldn't, but unfortunately, they usually don't. Even so, a whole library of software exists for a variety of different computers to help you generate everything from certificates to time lines to comparative graphs. I'll talk about two of these areas.

TimeLiner

Tom Snyder Productions has a product on the market called *TimeLiner*. It's simple and straightforward. It makes time lines — a day long, a week long, a year long, or many years long. You type in the information, in any order you like, and the program will arrange it, space it out proportionally, and give you a nice big banner or single page print out. At first look, most teachers see *TimeLiner* as a great tool for teaching kids about time lines. It is. Because it does all the proportional spacing for you, it allows students to focus on the information rather than getting bogged down in the mathematics of figuring the distance between each event. In addition, it allows kids to add or delete events (as well as merge time lines) without having to recalculate with each change. But because it has all these features, *TimeLiner* is also a great tool for you.

TimeLiner is great for teaching time lines, but it's also great for you.

Just a momentary digression. We've got to get out of the habit of reflexively viewing computers and software as materials exclusively for children. The computer revolution essentially bypassed the teacher as it rushed into the schools. Computers were for 10-year old pupils, not middle-aged instructors. Access for one group, however, should not exclude the other. In fact, a lot of programs that allow children to do neat things on the computer could likely be put to much better instructional use if

Think what a teacher could do with some of the computer tools given to kids.

45

A Tool for the Professional Teacher

placed in the hands of a good teacher. A student can take an interesting piece of software and do interesting things. A teacher can take that same piece of software and employ it to achieve his or her educational goals. Just something to keep in mind. End of digression.

Here are a couple of specific suggestions for what you can do with *TimeLiner*:

• Make illustrative time lines for your class. The most obvious use is in history where students grapple with understanding sequences of events and various cause and effect relationships. Such time lines, though, are also very helpful in literature. Books and stories are not always presented in sequential order. Plot time lines can help students better comprehend what they read. In addition, the proportional spacing feature can also be used to illustrate other relative values, besides time. Laurie Olafson, a teacher in Washington, offers these ideas:

TimeLiner's proportional spacing can be used to display relative values other than time.

First, I put the planets on the time line, using 0 for the sun, and putting in the miles from the sun without the zeros. Mercury was 36, Venus 67, earth 93, Mars 142, Jupiter 483, Saturn 887, Uranus 1783, Neptune 2794, Pluto 3666. The printout really shows the relationship of the planets and how far Pluto really is

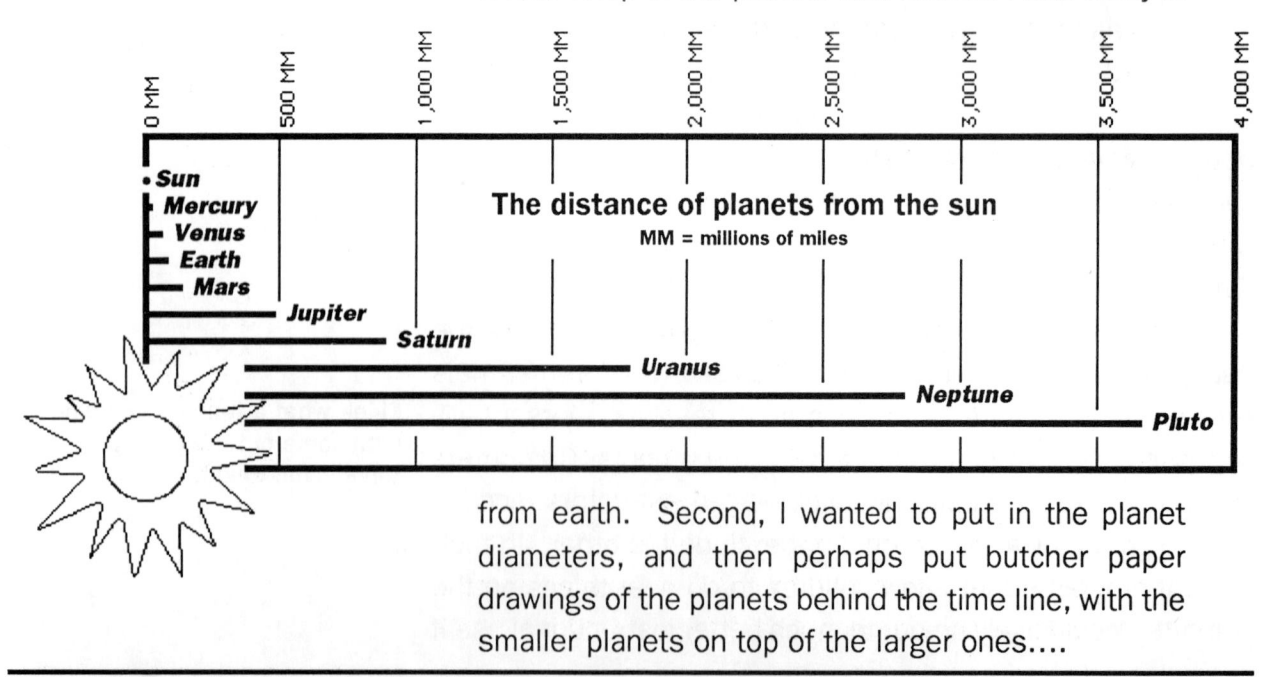

Try distance or size or temperature or...

The distance of planets from the sun
MM = millions of miles

from earth. Second, I wanted to put in the planet diameters, and then perhaps put butcher paper drawings of the planets behind the time line, with the smaller planets on top of the larger ones....

46

A Tool for the Professional Teacher

Other ideas that would show relative size would include the height of students in a class, number of calories in food, mileage run during running club, days of work enough to earn certain purchases.

I've tried some of these suggestions. They're fun, and they work.

• Make organizational time lines for yourself and your students. "I didn't know that was due today." "I thought we had another week for this project." Getting students, or almost anyone for that matter, to meet deadlines is a tough task. *TimeLiner* makes it easy to generate both short- and long-term schedules that can be posted for everyone to see. A teacher in New York made a giant time line of his curriculum and tacked it up around the room. Everyone knew what was coming and when. Of course, it wasn't long before they were off schedule. It's a good thing the program is easy to edit. A sixth grade class in Wyoming had a more creative scheduling idea. The kids, it seems, had a tough time remembering the deadlines for the annual science fair. With the help of *TimeLiner* and Dr. I.M. Madd, a wild cut-out character, they made their due dates. Madd was constructed with outstretched hands in which he held first monthly time lines and then daily ones that displayed the schedule for the approaching fair. According to the teacher, "the students not only remembered the deadlines but had fun reading them."

Helping students remember their deadlines

Social Studies Tool Kits

While *TimeLiner* gives you interesting ways to display information you have collected, another set of programs gives you the power to sift through lots of information in interesting ways. *The Social Studies Tool Kits: Our World* and *Our Nation* and *Time Patterns Tool Kit: U.S. History* each give you access to a huge number of data bases covering an incredible array of contemporary and historical topics. It's hard to think of an existing classroom analog for this kind of teacher activity. We all do (at least we all should do) research that goes beyond the textbook. As a teacher, I was constantly perusing supplementary materials for interesting anecdotes or data that I might use to

Information and the tools to use it

A Tool for the Professional Teacher

Before computers, I would never have attempted to sift through the tomes of data contained in these three packages.

Most data base programs call for obscure commands and key strokes.

These *Tool Kits* are dedicated and menu-driven.

What do you do with all this information?

enlighten my students on a particular lesson. But I would never have attempted to sift through the tomes of statistical data contained in and easily examined with these three packages.

Access to overwhelming amounts of information and the ability to manipulate it in diverse ways are among the several, and most commonly used, gifts brought to us by the computer. It's not that the machine makes it easier to do something we already do. The computer makes possible something we never before attempted. Getting a handle on this new power, however, can be a daunting experience. Most data base management programs for the education market have their own obstacles to overcome even before you get to the data. Their problem: they try to do too much. As open-ended tools they offer an incredible number of options, and it's easy to get lost and intimidated by the program's complexity. You end up spending much of your time learning how to use the program rather than accomplishing the desired tasks. On the other hand, dedicated software packages, those designed to accomplish specific objectives, provide you with easy access to a narrower, but often more powerful, set of options.

The Social Studies and *Time Patterns Tool Kits* fall into the latter category. Their straight-forward, menu-driven formats make them among the easiest data base programs I've ever seen. The pair of social studies packages include hundreds of data bases (280 on this nation alone) on the United States and the world. And despite their titles, either program can have valuable crossover applications in either science or math. The *Time Patterns* program draws on United States census data from 1790 to the present, allowing you to prepare graphically enlightening displays and carry out statistical analysis of valuable historical data. For those of you still wondering what you might do with all this information, let me give you some examples.

Think about the newspaper *USA Today*. Virtually everyday, the paper publishes some interesting graph about human behavior (how much TV kids watch, American eating habits, etc.), demographics (the best and worst places to live, causes of death, etc.), the physical world (world resource production, sizes of national parks, etc.), and so on. Each graph is either

A Tool for the Professional Teacher

a direct representation of some set of data or a weighted average of a combination of different sets of data. A quality of life index, for instance, might include data on crime, income, per pupil expenditures, taxes, and more. The depictions are fun to look at and often enlightening. We glance at them (something we can do with graphic representations that is impossible with raw numbers) and say, "Oh wow. That's interesting."

Create your own "Oh wow!" graphs with information available at your fingertips.

Simply put, *The Social Studies Tool Kits* allow you to create your own distillations of information using similar data. Let me give you an example. Imagine you're teaching a unit on birth, possibly as part of a health, sex education, or general science course. You want your students to understand, among other things, how scientists determine what factors influence fetal development. In fact, it would be great if they worked to uncover those factors themselves, rather than simply being told what they are. The *Tool Kits* can help. Look at the map below, for example. Using one of the data bases that comes with the *Our Nation Tool Kit*, I had the program print a map of the U.S. ranking states according to the percent of babies born with low birth weights. I noticed, as your students might and other observers already have, that the states with the highest percentages of babies with low birth weights seemed to all be located in the same southeastern region of the country. The bar graph makes the unequal distribution even clearer.

This is the kind of displayed information that can really get a group of students making some valuable inquiries. What causes this grouping? Why are there so many low birth weight babies in the south compared to the rest of the country? Is it coincidence? Climate? Social custom? Regional food? Economic status? *Time Patterns Tool Kit: U.S. History* enables you to seek similar

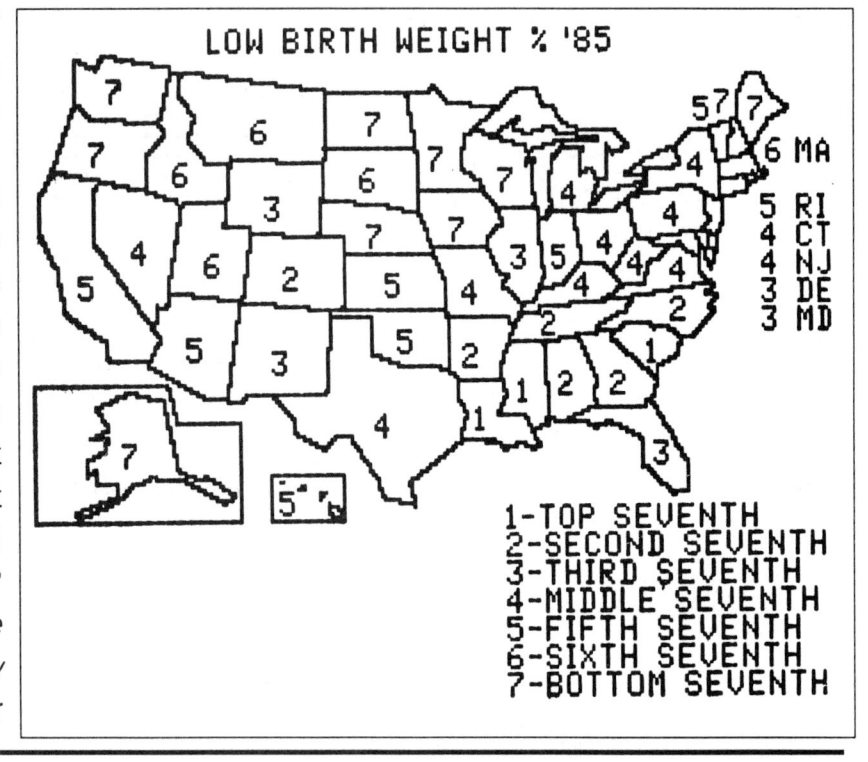

49

A Tool for the Professional Teacher

You provide the spark and direction for independent exploration.

patterns in the past. Are increases and decreases in infant mortality over time, for instance, related to changes in the availability of doctors or changes in dietary habits? You'll be amazed at the hypotheses your students will generate. Let them investigate. The library is a great resource and so are these tool kits. The computer has helped you provide the initial spark and direction, now your students can begin to use it as one of their tools for directed research. What correlations can they find? The possibilities are overwhelming.

```
       GRAPHED: LOW BIRTH WEIGHT % '85

MINN  I*****************************
ALAK  I****************************
N DK  I*****************************
N HP  I*****************************
OREG  I*****************************
MAIN  I*****************************
IOWA  I******************************
WISC  I*******************************
NEBR  I******************************
WASH  I******************************
IDAH  I*******************************
S DK  I*******************************
UTAH  I*******************************
MONT  I********************************
MASS  I*********************************
VRMT  I**********************************
CALF  I**********************************
KANS  I**********************************
ARIZ  I**********************************
RHOD  I***********************************
INDI  I***********************************
OKLA  I***********************************
HAWI  I************************************
PENN  I************************************
OHIO  I************************************
CONN  I************************************
MSRI  I************************************
MICH  I*************************************
N JR  I*************************************
TEXS  I*************************************
W VG  I**************************************<-------------SOUTH ATLANTIC
NEVA  I**************************************
N YK  I**************************************
VIRG  I***************************************<------------SOUTH ATLANTIC
KENT  I***************************************<------------EAST SOUTH CENTRAL
WYOM  I***************************************
N MX  I***************************************
ILLI  I****************************************
DELA  I*****************************************<----------SOUTH ATLANTIC
FLOR  I******************************************<---------SOUTH ATLANTIC
MARY  I******************************************<---------SOUTH ATLANTIC
COLO  I*******************************************
TENN  I********************************************<-------EAST SOUTH CENTRAL
N CR  I********************************************<-------SOUTH ATLANTIC
ARKN  I*********************************************
ALAB  I**********************************************<-----EAST SOUTH CENTRAL
GEOR  I***********************************************<----SOUTH ATLANTIC
S CR  I************************************************<---SOUTH ATLANTIC
LOUI  I*************************************************
MISS  I**************************************************<---EAST SOUTH CENTRAL
      !-------------------------!-------------------------!
      0                                                  8.8

EACH * STANDS FOR .18 PERCENT
. STANDS FOR LESS THAN 1% BUT GREATER THAN ZERO PERCENT
```

A Tool for the Professional Teacher

Organizing Ideas

In the original edition of this book, I began this section as follows: "I'm going to suggest a use for the computer that I myself don't employ." That opening is no longer true. Somewhere along the line I became hooked on the value of the computer as an organizational tool. I admit I fought hard to maintain my scattered scraps of paper approach to collecting and organizing information and ideas. But somehow it all changed. Let me explain.

Computers are very organized.

Now computers may not be all that wise, but they are very, very organized. They have to put each bit or byte away in its proper place. They perform tasks in the strictest order. They're never spontaneous, and they're only random when told to be so. You may even know some people who match this description.

Think about those folks for a moment. When I was a child, I thought parents and teachers were that way, always telling me to clean up my room and show my work. These people may not be that much fun at parties, but they perform a valuable service. Their organization can help you with yours. The computer can serve you in a similar fashion with your ideas.

Their organization can help you with yours.

Take lesson preparation, for example. For every unit I was about to teach, I would gather all the information, the content and the skills, that I wanted the students to acquire. I drew from the textbook, supplementary readings, old notes from college classes, handouts from presentations I'd attended, whatever I could get my hands on. I especially kept my eye out for interesting anecdotes that might add life and texture to each individual lesson. Then I'd sit and down organize everything. In what order should this information be presented? What's the best way to illustrate this point? Which skills should I highlight where? Where should I place the most emphasis? As I answered these questions, I would create a structure, an outline, which divided the whole unit into bite sized lessons.

I now use an outliner program to help me create these kind of outlines on the fly. Assume you're sitting at your computer, surrounded by books, papers, and notes. You reach for each piece of information and enter it, or a summary of it, into the computer (that was the investment I had never been able to drive myself to make, but it was worth it). As you compile your

Use an outliner to rearrange your ideas on the fly.

51

data, you give it order. You "promote" one idea and "demote" another, to use the language popular among outliners. You attach anecdotes to concepts and skills to activities. You rearrange and reorganize. You could, of course, perform all of these tasks on a word processor, but the outliner is dedicated to this purpose.

Hypertext offers another organizational scheme.

A more powerful, but still similar, application is available through what is commonly called "hypertext." This approach has been popularized by HyperCard and Apple's Macintosh computers. With hypertext, you can connect data of various sizes and types in a myriad of ways. To a discussion of Abraham Lincoln's image as president, you might, for example, attach excerpts from Lincoln's actual letters, digitized images of how he was portrayed in portraits and political cartoons, and anecdotes about his beard. If you wanted to change those connections for another class, you would merely reorganize. Once it's in the computer, you don't have to recreate from scratch every time you desire to make a change.

You have to make the initial investment to get the big payoff.

As with most new tools, from tennis rackets with big heads to VCRs and food processors, you have to make an initial investment of time to learn how the device works before you can really put it to work for you. In a sense, each piece of computer software, particularly general utilities, can be construed as a unique tool demanding time and patience. Once you get over the top of the learning curve, however, you may find a big payoff for your efforts.

Make the computer a part of what you already do.

Unfortunately, for many busy teachers that learning curve may look like an insurmountable mountain. The other side of it is unknown, and the time required for climbing it would take away from a long list of immediate needs. I very much appreciate that feeling, but, despite my skepticism about computers, I don't advocate ignoring the technology. Use it to help you with those immediate needs. Don't view the computer as something additional that you have to do. Make it a part of what you already do.

Another Day at the Office

Each one of the applications described in this chapter presents the computer as a tool for the preparation, management, and administration of the classroom. To really appreciate and expand upon these options, you have to picture the teacher as someone with an office, a set of tools, and responsibility for important tasks. When at the computer, the teacher, in this vision, is "at the office," analyzing data, planning future activities, projecting outcomes, and so on. When in the classroom, he or she is working "in the field," and that arena provides the context for the next section. Can a single computer assist the teacher in the field, where the action is fast and the risks high? The answer is yes. Read on to find out how.

Picture yourself as a professional, with an office and tools of the trade.

The Computer as a Presentation Tool

In the 1960s U.S. Steel ran an ad that extolled the coming computer revolution. Now some of you might be wondering why U.S. Steel would be promoting a computer terminal for every student as the solution for all our educational woes. You see, the computers of that revolution were large mainframes that required special housing and climate control. The terminals, too, were heavy-duty pieces of machinery. An instructional system utilizing this technological arrangement would require huge amounts of steel. The company wanted us to know that "the steel is ready when we are." I hope they're not still waiting.

a computer terminal for every student to solve all our educational woes

Anyway, this ad proclaimed individualized instruction as "the ultimate dream of effective education." Each child would work independently, individually paced by a set of software programs designed to meet his or her particular needs. It's a great vision, or is it? Aside from the fact that such an "intelligent" instructional system didn't exist then and doesn't exist now, I still don't envision individualized instruction as *my* ultimate dream of effective education.

"the ultimate dream of effective education"

I love groups. The notion of bringing thirty kids into the same room, putting headphones on them, and then having each one pretend the other twenty-nine aren't there seems not only unnatural but unhealthy. Much of what happens in school is social. Kids learn to get along and communicate with others. They learn about sharing and shared responsibility. They experience first-hand, and hopefully grow to appreciate, differences between individuals. We can't ignore that aspect of their education.

Much of what happens in school is social.

But even from the content side, I've always found groups a very important part of my students' education. I can't count the number of times I had planned the perfect lesson, the ideal organization of information, to lead my class into a developing

The Computer as a Presentation Tool

understanding of some concept only to be staring at a sea of blank faces. My presentation wasn't clicking with their mode of comprehension. I'd shift gears and try another approach, and then another. You must know what I mean. You're wondering, "How can they not understand this? It's all so clear to me." So I'd try to actively engage them, get them talking to one another. I wanted to hear how they were thinking and understanding. Their conversations usually enabled me to understand the way their minds were working so that I could somehow match it to what I wanted to teach. Sometimes one student's talk would enlighten another student's mind. You can never anticipate how some students make connections. That's why groups are so good. Thirty kids is such a great resource to share. Properly driven, students can learn a tremendous amount from each other.

When students discuss, you can hear how they're thinking.

So I'm sometimes surprised by those of you who are baffled, even frustrated, at the prospect or reality of having the computer brought into your classroom. "Great," you say. "Now we have one computer in our classrooms, but we still have thirty kids. What can we do with it?" But hey, you've only got one chalkboard, one overhead projector, one gradebook, one globe, one dazzling smile, one enlightening glance. And you use whatever of them you need to make your classroom work. A single computer in the classroom shouldn't be considered a resource shortage. It can help you in so many ways. Rather, the computer should be one of the essential weapons in a teacher's arsenal of ideas and activities to activate students.

So as you contemplate what to do with this machine that has invaded your inner

The Computer as a Presentation Tool

sanctum, that sits quietly in a corner of your room or on a cart down the hall, use those goals you set and magic moments you conjured up several pages ago. Remember those best classes to determine how you will use the computer to make them happen again. How can it assist you in recreating your most cherished experiences in school? The possibilities are endless.

Use your magic moments in the classroom to direct computer use.

To help you think through these possibilities, imagine your classroom as a stage. On it you and your students perform a variety of different kinds of plays, within which you take different parts. Sometimes you're strictly the director while the students put on the show. Other times, it's basically a solo performance with the class as participant/audience. Occasionally, a number of vignettes occur simultaneously, as small groups of pupils work independently. For each type of play, the computer can take an invaluable supporting role. It can play the smart chalkboard in the hands of the solo performer; it can act as the discussion generator for large group extravaganzas; and it can be the small group activator for multiple performances. This chapter and the following two present the computer in each of these three roles, starting with what we call *the smart chalkboard*.

Think of the classroom as a stage.

The Smart Chalkboard

Think about how you currently use your chalkboard in your classroom — illustrating ideas, presenting information, demonstrating complex formulae, managing your students. Now dream about what you'd like the chalkboard to be able to do — draw and re-draw as you command, animate important movements, keep up with your presentation of material. Connecting your computer to some sort of large screen display can help turn these dreams into reality. Big screen attachments come in many forms and at many prices. The most expensive (into the thousands of dollars) device projects in beautiful full color, but it is too pricey to become a commonplace classroom tool. Of growing popularity are LCD palettes (still several hundred dollars), such as the PC Viewer. These thin peripherals turn your computer display into a sort of electronic transparency which sits on top of your overhead projector. If you already have televisions in the school, even old ones, a third alternative is an

Big screen options for your computer

57

The Computer as a Presentation Tool

A glimpse at my experiences in the classroom

Never turn your back on your students.

One day, I turned my back...

RF Modulator for $30. This box attaches to the antenna connection on the back of your TV. Then all you have to do is plug the video cable from your computer into the box and set the television channel to 2 or 3. With an additional small cable, called a y-splitter, you can send the video output to two places at once, a large screen for the class and a small monitor for you.

At the simplest level these projection alternatives allow you to take much of the software designed for one person at the computer and display it to everyone at once. Be aware, though, that not all one-on-one software lends itself to such an easy transition to group use. It's got to have a very simple interface. Let me illustrate with a story.

Among my first teaching experiences was a fairly inner-city high school in New Haven, Connecticut (a teacher was shot and killed that year at one of the other high schools in the city). I was finishing up at Yale, and I did my practice teaching at this bizarre school without windows. It had all interior classrooms — no glass anywhere. And the practice teaching wasn't really practice. It was more like sink or swim. They gave me three classes to teach, and then turned around and basically said, "See you in nine weeks." I was pretty much on my own. As far as the kids were concerned, the name of the teacher on their schedule was a mistake. I was their instructor. All in all, I loved it. I couldn't have asked for a more, shall we say, rich experience. I learned a lot very quickly.

For instance, when I first started I met these teachers who wrote on the chalkboard backwards. What I mean is, they had learned how never to turn their backs on their students and still draw legibly with chalk. It was a pretty impressive bit of contortion. I laughed. I was naive. At the time, I figured there was no such thing as a bad student, only bad teachers. That's before I had taught.

Then, in one of my classes, not all of them, but in one, I found out how natural selection in the schools had left these teachers with that arm-twisting survival trait. The class was the one that had 40 or so names on the student roster of which no more than 20 ever appeared. The one that didn't really have a curriculum. A number of the kids couldn't read or write. I was supposed to occupy them for 45 minutes. If they learned something, that was a great extra. The main goal, however, was to keep them in one place for that block of time. I had such tremendous expectations. Finally, one day, I turned to draw something relatively elaborate on the chalkboard. When I turned back to face the class, I saw the door on the side of the classroom open. A third of the class was gone. A second third, that sat in the front and made very few movements to indicate they were alive, continued to do that. And a final third was bunched in the back of the room deeply involved in some activity. I don't know exactly what they were doing, but I'm pretty sure it was illegal.

Kids long for distractions.

Now, you may not experience such an extreme reaction when you turn your back on your students, but you do know that kids long for distractions. When you're in the middle of a lesson and someone knocks on the door with a brief message from the office your students do not sit on the edge of their seats anxiously awaiting your return. "Gee, I can't wait for Mr. Dockterman to get back and finish that point." They start to drift. I still meet teachers who prefer to use the overhead projector over the chalkboard for the very reason that it doesn't draw them away from their class. They don't have to turn their backs on their kids.

Computer programs that demand constant attention, such as arcade-like software, or that require complicated keystroke combinations, like elaborate simulations or data base managers, can easily draw you into their enticing microworlds and away from your students. It's difficult to keep your class riveted with your head buried in the keyboard. You either have to learn how to type backgrounds or seek software that allows you to teach and use the computer at the same time. It's like singing and playing the piano. It's much more powerful when the two happen together.

It's like singing and playing the piano.

An Earth Science Lesson

Take *GeoWorld*, for example. Here's a program, an exploratory simulation that really is designed for use by one or two students sitting together at a computer. But the interface is so simple — spacebar, arrow keys, and Return are the only keys you ever press — that it easily translates to the big screen. In fact, I often prefer using it with a large group. *GeoWorld*

***GeoWorld* easily translates to the big screen.**

The Computer as a Presentation Tool

an enormous data base

simulating a geologist searching for oil...

...and the world and all the data are real

I love it when students request to use reference materials.

breaks the world into little blocks, 1 1/2° latitude by 1 1/2° longitude. For each one of those blocks, the program knows the actual amount of fifteen different resources found there, not to mention the specific geological formation of that area. So for, say, a small section of South Africa, the software knows the major rock types, the structure of the underlying strata, and the estimated amount of aluminum, chromium, cobalt, coal, copper, gold, iron, lead, manganese, nickel, oil, silver, tin, uranium, and zinc in that location. It's an incredible data base, but that's not the best part. All that data is imbedded in a simulation. The information is not merely given to you, you have to discover it, just like a geologist would.

Picture an earth science class (although there are a number of social studies applications, as well). You want to teach your kids, among other things, how certain resources are found in certain geological environments. You boot up *GeoWorld*, choose to search for oil (that's one I know something about), and then confront a map of the world in the center of which you see a flashing box that measures 20° latitude x 20° longitude. You ask the class, "Where should we go look for oil?" If the group is like a number I've visited recently, they'll want to go to Australia. Some may even be able to point it out on the map. (For whatever reason, it's a hot continent, but if Crocodile Dundee III doesn't appear soon, it may quickly fade from popularity.) A few members of the class, however, may suggest alternatives. How do you decide? How do geologists know where to begin looking for particular resources?

In the program, you can travel to different parts of the world, testing out your hunches, but it's not a very efficient way to proceed. It won't be long before your kids ask for some guidance. "Can we use the reference books?" I love it when students request to use reference materials; it doesn't happen often enough. So you turn to the encyclopedia or the textbook or even the newspaper. The Persian Gulf area looks like an oil-rich region, so, after locating it on a political map (another outside reference), you choose to head there. Zooming in on the location you choose gives you a close-up look at the 20° x 20° block.

Doing a geochemical test, which performs a general survey

The Computer as a Presentation Tool

of the area to determine the likelihood of finding the designated resource, confirms that you're in the right place. Now, where should you drill for oil? You can wildcat, randomly mining 1 1/2° x 1 1/2° quadrants, and you might get lucky. A few empty efforts, however, will soon convince your students to seek a more systematic approach. Taking a core sample, which displays the rock type and raw minerals found in different quarters of the larger block, will narrow your search. If your kids have done their homework, they'll know to look for marine fossils in the lists on the screen. Such fossils are the footprints for the organic materials that, as they slowly deteriorated under water and sediment, produced oil. If your kids don't know, it's a fantastic opportunity to explain the process in a relevant context. Try creating this kind of exploratory environment with a piece of chalk.

Try creating this kind of exploratory environment in your classroom with a piece of chalk.

You're not done yet. You've found a place where oil is likely to have been produced, but is it also a place where oil is likely to have been trapped? What's to keep the oil from seeping away into or out of the earth? How do you know you'll find a big pool of resource waiting to be pumped to the surface? You'll have to take a look. You use the program to take a cross-sectional slice of the area in question. You see geological diagrams, just like the ones real geologists use. To the novice, these diagrams may mean very little. But with some background (and with the help of Resource Information Sheets like the one on the right), you can begin to recognize symbols for

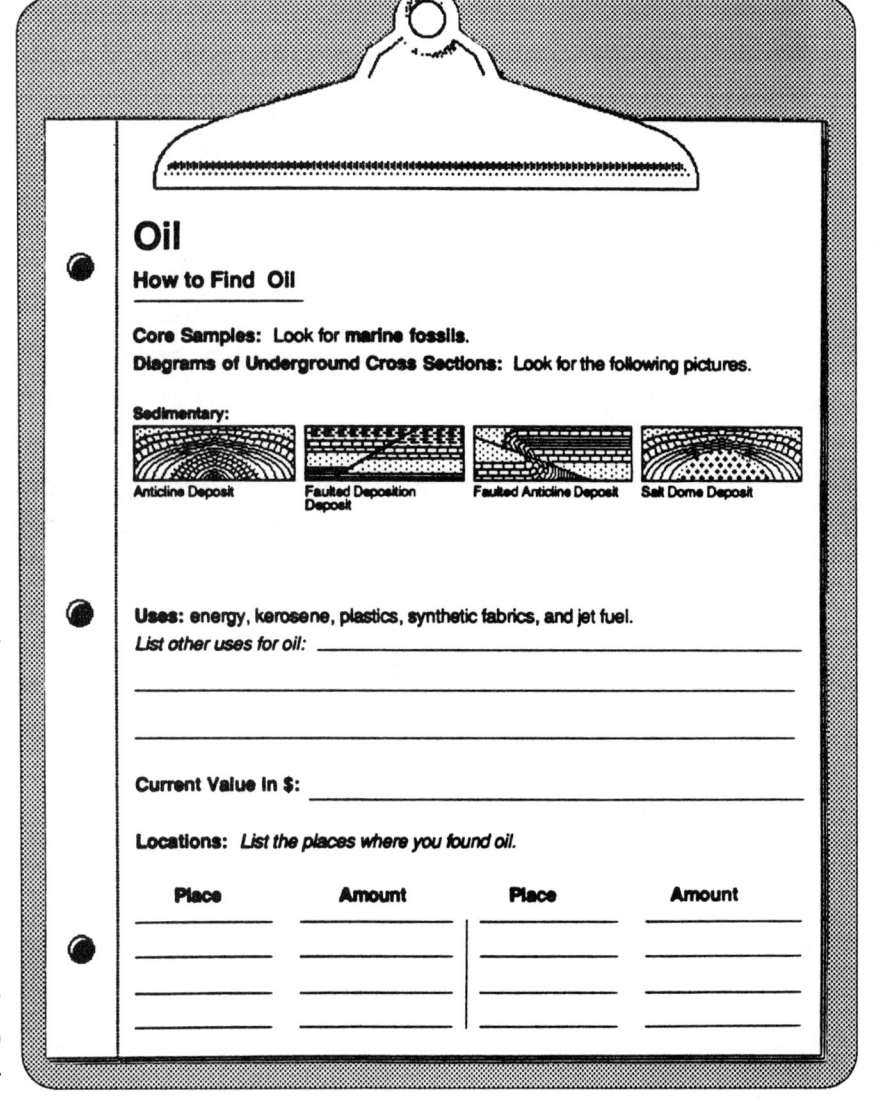

Oil
How to Find Oil

Core Samples: Look for **marine fossils**.
Diagrams of Underground Cross Sections: Look for the following pictures.

Sedimentary:

Anticline Deposit   Faulted Deposition Deposit   Faulted Anticline Deposit   Salt Dome Deposit

Uses: energy, kerosene, plastics, synthetic fabrics, and jet fuel.
List other uses for oil: _____

Current Value in $: _____

Locations: *List the places where you found oil.*

Place	Amount	Place	Amount

The Computer as a Presentation Tool

metamorphic, igneous, and sedimentary rocks. What you're looking for is a sedimentary deposit with a pocket to trap oil, like anticlines, faults, or salt domes. (Earth science teachers are probably drooling with excitement at this description. The rest of you may not share that enthusiasm.) Mine one of those deposits. If you've done a good job, you should get a message that you just discovered so many thousands of kilotons of oil. Mine another spot, and then another. At some point stop and display your record. You'll see how much of the world's known reserves you've uncovered so far. That's always a great "Oh wow" for students. If you've been mining the Persian Gulf area, you'll see how such a small area can be so influential in international politics. I'm getting off the earth science track, but you can see how this kind of group discovery can open up a number of other doors for you and your students to explore.

This kind of group discovery can open up a number of other doors.

You can do more with *GeoWorld*, but not necessarily in the one-computer classroom. All the data you uncover — the deposit size, its percentage of the world's known reserves, its location, and its geological surroundings — can all be saved and then transferred to *AppleWorks*, the popular data base management program, for further examination. How much oil, for example, is in the Middle East versus North America? Does oil tend to be found within a certain longitudinal or latitudinal range? While interesting, these questions are hard to examine as a whole class using one computer and *AppleWorks*. You can do it if you're adept at *AppleWorks*' keystrokes, if you're patient with small text on the screen, and if you're willing to turn your back on your class for short periods. Otherwise, these questions are great for independent exploration by individuals or pairs of students. So send them to the computer lab or to the library. You've primed them. You've used what aspects of the program you can to illustrate important points and generate excitement and interest. Let the students do the rest.

The data you discover can then be examined with *Appleworks*.

Math Problem-Solving and Math Exploration

Several math packages that translate nicely to the large projection method are worth mentioning. The first, which is actually a series, is the *McGraw-Hill Mathematics Problem-Solving Courseware* for grades 5-8. (It's a catchy title, isn't it?)

Word problems for the whole class.

Each package in the series offers kids a graphically compelling, real life context in which they can practice working with meaningful word problems. The computer does all the computation while the students concentrate on highlighting the important information and organizing the problem. In its one-on-one application, the software allows individual students to explore large environments at their own pace and in their own way. A record-keeping feature provides the teacher with information on how each student is progressing with various types of problems. Used with an LCD device for whole group exploration, you might lose the individual pacing, but you gain some valuable group interaction.

Take the grade 7 package, The Secret of Vincent's Museum, for instance. It's one of my favorites. Your class takes the role of an investigative reporter seeking to uncover the reason for the uncanny rapid rise to success of the Vincent Museum. You begin at the door of the museum on the night of a big costume celebration. Using the arrow keys (again, a very simple interface) you move through the museum, meeting and talking to various characters. The 3-D graphics, by the way, are incredible, and their minimalistic style looks good even through a gray-scale LCD projection. Each character, not surprisingly, has problems for you to solve, as well as clues to the solution of the bigger mystery. You can have a fun class discussion just about which direction to head next.

Your class takes the role of an investigative reporter.

Each character has problems as well as information about the bigger mystery.

When you step up to one of the personalities in the museum, he or she will talk to you. Be careful of Janet Whitmore, the museum's director. Once she gets your ear, you can't shut her up. She loves to talk about herself, especially about how great she is, how she turned the old 3-room Vincent's Museum into a huge success. A few years ago, she'll remind you, Smedley's Museum used to get all the business — 56,788 visitors a year. This year, Janet claims, Vincent's will draw three times that number at $1.75 per person. She wants us to figure out what that means in terms of total dollars. Aha, a math problem. Now while we're listening to Janet, all I have to do is press Return and whatever text that appears on the screen will automatically be copied to a special built-in math note pad. I usually let the class decide what they think is important. Then, when I press N, I'll

You set up the problem, the computer does the computation.

The Computer as a Presentation Tool

see a list of all the information we chose to record along with a display of possible math operations — + - x ÷ — to perform. Sometimes the information selected is insufficient to solve the problem; sometimes it's far more than we need. In any case, when we've collected the necessary data, we must select the appropriate operation and plug in the right numbers in the right places. The computer will then complete the computation.

The problem Janet has presented has one correct answer, but there's more than one possible way to reach it. We could first multiply the number of visitors by 3, and then multiply that product times the price per person. On the other hand, we could rearrange the order of those operations. Either path will lead to the same conclusion. With a group of students offering suggestions, you'll hear those different routes. The kids will see, and be able to discuss, that there's more than one way to solve a problem. That's a very valuable lesson, and one that is often missing from one-on-one work.

One answer but lots of possible ways to get to it

The McGraw-Hill math programs provide a nice ongoing group activity throughout the semester or year. As you progress through each mystery (the 5th grade level takes place in a hotel, 6th grade in a toy store, 7th grade in a museum, and 8th grade in a seaside town), the demands of the problems follow the general math curriculum for those grades. You can also concentrate on more general problem solving skills, as your students organize information to solve the larger mystery.

It's a nice ongoing activity.

In contrast to the directed experiences of the aforementioned math mysteries, several packages come in the form of much more open-ended tools. Programs such as the *Geometric Supposer* and *Interactive Physics* are impressive exploratory pieces of software that you can use to improve and illustrate your own presentations. Let me offer a couple of examples.

Open-ended math and physics chalkboards

Suppose you are introducing your students to isosceles triangles. Traditionally, you would lay out the rules for such a geometric figure and then give some examples. Math textbooks, in particular, are great at defining rules or theorems or formulae, and then asking students at the end of the chapter to apply what was just defined. I myself managed straight A's in math by mastering the technique of plugging the right numbers into the right places in equations that I did not understand. Developing

64

some of that missing understanding is, I believe, a good thing. So let's reverse the process and construct the rules ourselves from some initial examples. To follow this approach I need the *Geometric Supposer*, a big screen, and a chalkboard.

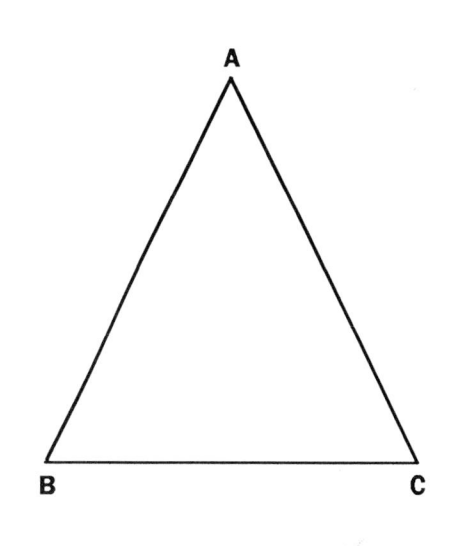

The *Supposer* has a relatively straight-forward on-screen menu, and I'll begin by simply typing N for a new triangle. I then choose isosceles for the type and voila, I have triangle ABC. Already the program does something I find difficult to accomplish with just chalk and board; it draws a perfect isosceles or equilateral or right-angled or random triangle with incredible ease and speed. "Now, what features," I might ask the class, "make this isosceles triangle different from just any old triangle?" We might take some measurements. A menu displays our options. We build a list of data as we measure angles, line segments, area, perimeter, point to line distances, and more.

As we survey the information we have accumulated, I ask, "What can you now tell me about isosceles triangles?" "Nothing," will hopefully be the answer. One example dose not a pattern (let alone a rule) make. Fine. A press of a button gives me another isosceles triangle. This one looks different. Are patterns beginning to emerge? Gradually the group will generate a set of isosceles triangle rules that I will write on the chalkboard. Are we done yet? Hardly. Now we must test our rules. Let's look at some non-isosceles triangles, and so on.

Throughout this experience the teacher simultaneously follows and guides the group, allowing them to confirm or disconfirm their own ideas as they are nudged toward understanding. The software serves the teacher much the way a traditional chalkboard would, except that this equipment always draws straight lines and calculates on the fly.

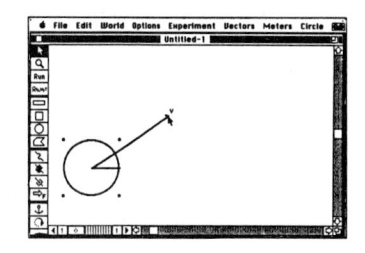

Another program in this genre, *Interactive Physics*, is worth mentioning because it brings the additional feature of animation to the smart chalkboard world. Here's a quick physics example (one that even I can understand) about gravity that barely scratches the surface of what this package offers. You won't believe how easy it is. Select the circle from the drawing palette and create a ball. Then click in the middle of the ball and stretch out a velocity arrow to indicate the direction and force with which you will throw the ball. Then click run. The ball will travel through

The Geometric Supposer

The teacher simultaneously follows and guides the group.

Interactive Physics

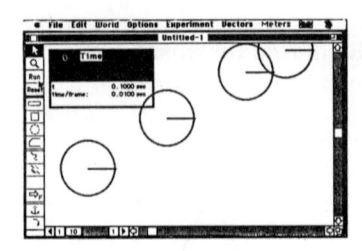

Open-ended can be dangerous.

Some one-on-one programs translate better to the big screen than others.

space, rising and falling as gravity returns it to "earth. But what would happen if the ball were thrown on the moon where gravity is much lower than on earth? No problem. Let's find out. You can set the gravity, air resistance, size of the world, traits of the ball, and much more. You can activate meters and measures to chart movement. You can draw a car, put a passenger in it, and send it crashing into a wall. *Interactive Physics* offers an incredibly powerful animating and measuring tool for illustrating concepts you have previously only been able to describe.

Both of these programs, and others like them, are incredibly flexible tools. In fact, that feature makes them at once attractive and difficult, even dangerous, to use in a classroom setting. Frankly, open-endedness can be a problem. You simply have too many choices. Unless you have a clear understanding of how the software operates, as well as a well-defined agenda for your lesson, it's very easy to get pulled away from your plan. Indeed, some of the attractive options in the program can actually become distractions. Unlike the bare but incredibly flexible chalkboard, the enticing palette of a program like *Interactive Physics* can draw you into following unexpected paths. This kind of random exploration isn't necessarily bad, but it isn't always what you want. Nor is it always what you have time for. These are just additional factors to keep in mind as you examine software possibilities for your own classroom.

Some of the features in the above-mentioned earth science and math programs clearly lend themselves to more independent use by students. Keep those design features in mind as you attempt to translate these and other pieces of software to the big screen. Don't force it. If some one-on-one software fits your needs and style in the one-computer classroom, take advantage of it. If not, don't use it because it's there. Be patient. People in the industry are beginning to take this presentational use of the computer seriously, and some software is already being designed specifically for this approach.

Group Review

One of those programs is *All Star Drill*. It's made to help you with a traditional chalkboard/group activity: group review. I used to play Jeopardy. At the end of a unit or before a major test,

The Computer as a Presentation Tool

I'd create a Jeopardy game. On the chalkboard I'd write the titles of five categories and lists of increasing values under each heading. I then held in my hand five sheets of paper with the answers and correct questions ("please make sure it's in the form of a question") for each corresponding value and category. I broke the class into various teams and then ran the game. It was fun. The kids had a good time. We covered a lot of information, and I could see and hear where the students had gaps of understanding. That's one of the advantages of reviewing in a group. You, as teacher, get to be a part of the process. As you sense miscomprehension, even when the student responses are correct, you can intervene and probe in meaningful ways.

All Star Drill helps you turn this kind of group review into a baseball game. Here's how it works: Divide your students into two teams. Let each team pick a name for itself and maybe even design a mascot. Sometime before you plan to do the review (give yourself a day or two to play the game), type into the program the team names and players. Also, use the built-in editor to create the set of review questions. You have the option of either open-ended or multiple choice questions. I prefer the open-ended type. They're easier to create, give me more leeway in judging student responses, and allow me to control the pace more easily. Some teachers, however, opt for the multiple choice mode. One teacher in South Carolina explained that he finds the multiple choice option great for preparing kids for the standardized tests they face regularly in their academic careers. *All Star Drill*, he says, provides a non-threatening environment to develop the skills for successfully analyzing this type of question. Consequently, he devotes as much time to the content as he does to the process of separating likely answers from unlikely ones. Both approaches have merit. You can use them as you see fit.

When you're finally ready to play, the computer will call up the players, present the questions, keep track of the action and scoring, record individual statistics (cumulative, from game to game), but leave you in charge of the class. The game play displayed on the big screen — line drawings of fielding and hitting efforts — are very much fun. The program also includes

All Star Drill **is made specifically for the smart chalkboard.**

I used to play Jeopardy.

All Star Drill **turns group review into a baseball game.**

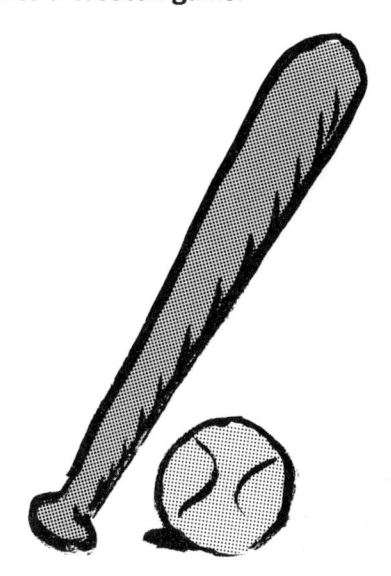

The program has features to help you keep everyone involved.

The Computer as a Presentation Tool

The computer as classroom secretary

some interesting features to help keep everyone in the class, particularly the team not up to bat, paying attention. If there's a runner on base and the player at bat gives an incorrect response, the computer will randomly pick a player from the other team, the one in the field, and ask for the correct answer. The program, however, won't repeat the question. The fielders have to be on their toes. If the fielder supplies the correct answer, the runner will be held at his or her current base. If the fielder is wrong, the runner will advance. A certain amount of peer pressure, prompted by the competitive spirit of the game, reinforces student attentiveness. Overall, *All Star Drill*, simply but effectively, turns the computer into a classroom secretary to help you manage a typical group activity.

Group Grammar & the Random Student Picker

a classroom management tool

Another package specifically designed with the large screen and large groups in mind is aptly titled *Group Grammar*. Shortly after booting up the software you see special one-computer classroom features. One of the opening screens asks you to type in the number of students in your class. This request sets in motion the Random Student Picker, a feature that appears in several TSP packages. Each student in your class is given a number from 1 to the total you input into the program. Then, whenever a decision needs to be made, a suggestion given, or a conflict resolved, you merely type P and the computer will randomly pick one of your students. Selecting a student may seem like a trivial task that teachers regularly perform, but picking a student can easily be construed as *picking on* a student. Somehow the arbitrary, objective nature of the computer invites less resistance than the directed call of the teacher. Let me describe the feature's use in this language arts program to illustrate.

in search of the most amazing adjective

Group Grammar takes a story and presents it in manageable phrases which allow you to introduce and review grammar types. The computer is connected to a large screen display. The program presents a grammar type, let's say an adjective, for the class to find on page 1 of the story. The text of page 1 appears broken down on the screen into 9 phrases. One of the

The Computer as a Presentation Tool

phrases is highlighted; that's your starting point. It looks something like this (from a story that comes on the disk):

It started	a million years ago	when a distant star
exploded.	A chunk of rock	flew through space
for almost a million years	before it landed	on Uncle Bill.

After reading the page aloud to the class, you tell your students to find the indicated grammar type, in this case adjectives. They have 4 moves to hit as many as possible. You move by pushing an arrow key toward a neighboring phrase. The next page will ask for a different grammar type as the story continues. The more matches you make, the more points the class receives.

Both the game and the story itself (what happens to Uncle Bill?) provide motivation for student involvement and attention. Now the fun starts. Where are the adjectives? One student wants to head down to "million years." Another suggests moving right to "chunk of rock" and then onto "distant star." You might hear some misconceptions. You and other students correct improper definitions. It gets a little loud, and it's time for a decision. You press P and the random student picker does its imitation of the state lottery before finally displaying number 12. Everyone quiets and turns to that student. What should we do? Fortunately, the selected student has heard the previous discussion and suggestions. If he has no other ideas, he can always play off of one of those. The process continues for four moves. Did students get points as they expected? Did they encounter any surprises? Page 2 follows with another grammar type and more story.

A built-in editor lets teachers set the grammar types they wish to cover and even create their own stories. You are definitely in control of the content. The computer is merely performing a number of useful management functions — running a game, keeping your place, helping with classroom control, etc. — that free you to listen more carefully and interact more appropriately with your students.

An enticing story and the game provide context and motivation.

putting the Random Student Picker to work

A built-in editor gives you control.

InnerBodyWorks **is designed for a number of classroom settings.**

A group tour through the human body.

Biology and Health

Here's one last program that fits into the category of smart chalkboard: *Dr. Know-it-all's InnerBodyWorks*. This package (actually there are two versions, one for elementary and one for junior and senior high) has been designed to operate in a variety of modes in the classroom. In fact, one of the opening menus asks you to choose which approach to follow: the big screen field trip, which requires an LCD palette or big screen monitor; the single player game for use in a computer lab; or the double team game, for two groups competing at one computer. It's the first mode that I wish to describe here.

Basically, *InnerBodyWorks* creates the context for either an open-ended or a directed tour through the human body. At the outset, you choose Hypertour or Game mode. In Hypertour you can follow the body's interconnected systems or jump from place to place as you desire. Trace the flow of blood through the heart with a useful visual display, or leap from elbow to knee in an examination of joints. A Get Information feature gives you immediate access to descriptions of your current location.

The game mode, on the other hand, provides more direction for movement from place to place. The computer tells the class its starting location in the body (right ventricle, left tibia, stirrup, gluteus maximus, or wherever) and four hot spots for the group to visit during its turn. The hot spots, which are other locations in the body, are described in clue form. For example, these four messages might appear: 1. Go to the master hormone gland located in the brain; 2. Proceed to the bone commonly called the jawbone; 3. Travel to the sacrum; and 4. Go to the site that closes to prevent blood from entering the trachea. (The main differences between the elementary and upper grade versions of the program have to do with anatomical detail and technical naming.)

Armed with their beginning and hot spot locations, the members of the class then turn to their information and body map booklets to decipher the clues and to plan their moves. The goal is to visit as many hot spots as possible per turn, moving step-by-step through the body's interconnecting parts and systems. Each location is visually displayed and comes with a list of connecting parts. In addition, at certain places you can jump from one system, say the circulatory, to another, such as the digestive. Each hot spot you hit is worth more points than the last, and a series of successful runs through the body could earn the class a first-level prize: the Copper Kidney Award.

In search of the Copper Kidney Award

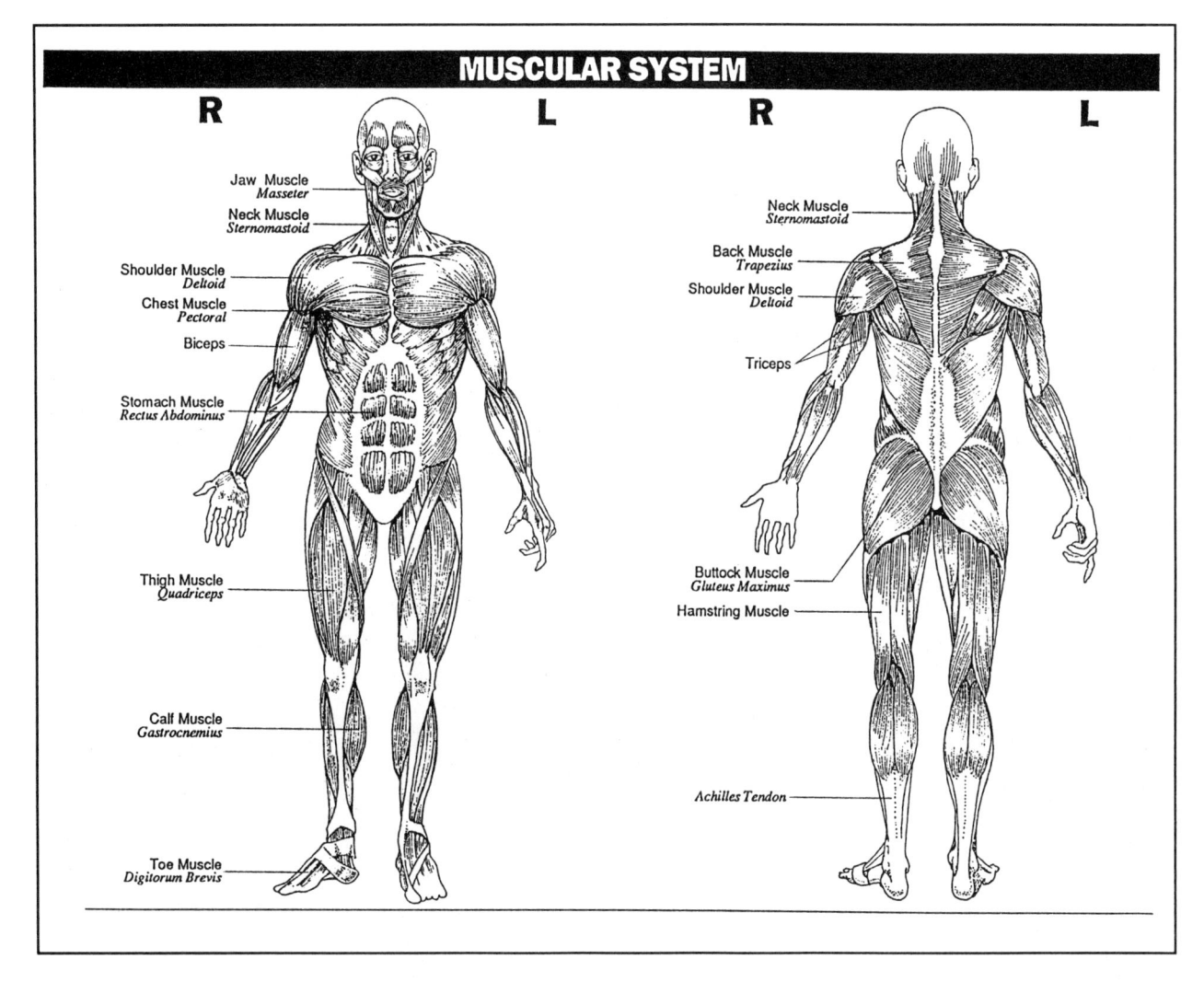

The discussions and debates about which path to follow from one hot spot to the next are dynamic, fun, and filled with

MUSCULAR SYSTEM

valuable content. The program even has a few classroom management tools built-in to ease your job of running the classroom. The Random Student Picker, for instance, helps you keep the group on task. A simple press of a button will randomly select someone in the class to answer a question or choose a route. It's just one simple example of the many ways a computer can assist you in whole group instruction.

Special features for classroom management

The Computer as a Presentation Tool

Start with something simple and straight forward.

In Search of the Generic Smart Chalkboard

Each of the products described in this chapter is tied either to a particular content area or to a specific type of classroom activity. None, by itself, is a true smart chalkboard. Not too long ago, I was quoted in a magazine as saying that TSP was working on "smart chalkboard" applications. For the next several months, I received numerous calls inquiring when this new program, *The Smart Chalkboard*, would be complete.

It certainly is an attractive idea — a generic smart chalkboard that always draws perfect circles in math, sets cars in motion at designated speeds in physics, correctly deploys soldiers at the Battle of Antietam in history, and automatically diagrams sentences in language arts. It sounds wonderful, but it isn't real. In fact, programs that attempt to satisfy needs in all these areas quickly run the risk of becoming cumbersome. They certainly become dangerous.

In general, I suggest you seek simple, straightforward applications. At least, that's where you should start, unless, of course, you can type behind your back without taking your eyes off your students.

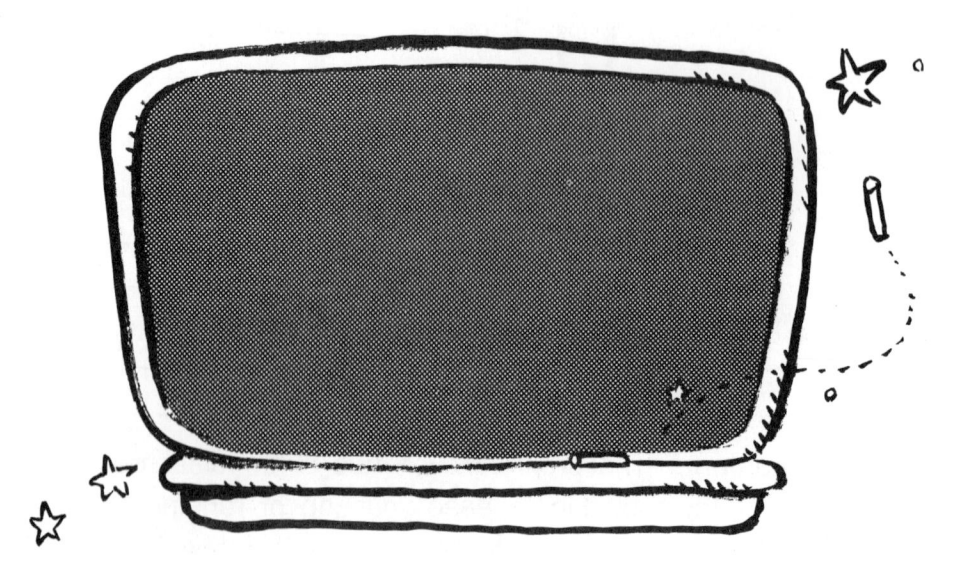

The Computer as a Discussion Generator

As I mentioned earlier, I'm a big fan of constructive conversation in the classroom. The active interchange of ideas, the articulation of thought processes, and the challenge of conflicting opinions make classroom discussion an invaluable exercise. Generating that discussion, however, isn't always that easy. I remember when I was teaching during the Iranian hostage crisis in 1980. I wanted to get my students, especially the ones in my World Cultures class, involved in the situation. To spark some thoughtful discussion, I'd tell them, "You're Jimmy Carter. The hostages are in Iran. What do you do?" I'll bet you can guess their response. What would a typical group of ninth graders say? Yep, "Nuke 'em!" So then I caution, "I don't know if that will get the hostages back safely or not."

And the kids all say, "Nuke 'em!"

It's tough, and it's typical. Everywhere I speak across the country I ask teachers what their kids would say in this situation. The response is always, 100 percent of the time, the same. "Blow them up." This commonness among adolescent American culture is reassuring in a disturbing sort of way. As a teacher, what do you do? I often found myself up in front of the group simultaneously pushing and pulling. I wanted them to give me their original thoughts and ideas, but not those thoughts and ideas.

And even if you succeed in getting them going in a thoughtful way, it's still very difficult to sustain. It's hard work, managing thirty kids and a head full of content at the same time. As a teacher, when I used to get observed by the head of the department or someone from the administration, I always wanted to put on a show that included one of those dynamic discussions I described in chapter 2. I wanted to impress, especially during my first two years. My kids could sense my nervous anxiety when an "evaluator" walked into the room.

Discussions are tough to create and even tougher to maintain.

The Computer as a Discussion Generator

A great class is incredibly satisfying...but exhausting.

I worked with Tom Snyder to design this series as something I would use in my own classroom.

Many would try to come to my rescue, hamming it up with long, ineloquent speeches and superficial criticisms of others' comments. Together, though, we'd generate something worthwhile, even exciting. I'd be prompting, listening, correcting, prompting some more. What new bit of information can I throw out that will confuse and enlighten them? What question should I ask next? And to whom? I was also trying to watch each student. Who's passing notes or fading out of the discussion?

At the end, I'd be exhausted but satisfied. The class would march out, and I'd flop into the chair next to the observer. He'd say, "That was great, but did you notice that one kid in the corner was really not involved..." I'd feel guilty. I'd tried to notice, but maybe I missed him. Or maybe I did notice but got distracted in my mind before I had a chance to act. It was easy for the observer to observe, but much more demanding to participate and observe and control. As odd as this may sound, a single computer on your desk can actually help you generate and manage these kinds of discussions more easily.

Decisions, Decisions

Decisions, Decisions is the name of a series of role-playing software packages designed specifically to help you generate informed discussion and decision-making in the classroom using only one computer. The program does have a small group option for managing a cooperative learning environment (I'll describe that option more thoroughly in the next chapter), but I'm going to describe the teacher-centered, whole class approach as I usually use it. You don't need a display system, although it's fine to use one. I usually just employ a single computer sitting on my desk or on a cart in the front of the room. The screen can be facing the kids or not. I tend to suggest letting the students look at the screen, even if they can't read what's on it. At least they can tell that something's happening. It adds to the drama. I then act as the interface between the class and the machine. That position makes it easier for me to orchestrate the discussions.

I usually start a *Decisions, Decisions* simulation, however, before I bring in the computer. Each title comes with its own set of student reference books, and I distribute one to each member of the class. If I want to prep the students for the issues they'll face in the program, I'll use the lessons in the teacher's guide to introduce appropriate background information even before distributing the books. Sometimes, though, I'll use the context of the simulation to introduce the desired material. My approach varies from group to group.

The first pages of the reference books describe the situation in which the students are enrolling. Depending on my time commitment, I will ask the class to read those pages as a first homework assignment. Otherwise, I might have one of the students read them aloud in class. In each title, the situation reflects recurring issues in history, science, or contemporary life. In *Immigration: Maintaining the Open Door*, for example, the class becomes President of the United States facing the option of running for reelection after one term in office. The primaries loom ahead, and the group must confront challenges for the nomination from within the party. Do they want to be President again?

As they contemplate their political future, they are interrupted by a crisis demanding their immediate attention. Boat loads of refugees, tens of thousands of them, are about to land on the shores of the country. In fact, they're about to land in the main city of the state in which you must fight one of your first primary battles. The citizens of the town and the state are concerned. As far as you know, these uninvited refugees come from a war-torn, poverty-stricken part of the world. Some are coming to the United States escaping political (often Communist) oppression. Others seek a brighter economic future. In either case, they carry few possessions, speak little or no English, have no essential skills, and represent the first wave of immigrants to the United States from that part of the globe. They have no one, no network of fellow country-persons, waiting to receive them. However, volunteer groups across the country are rapidly trying to arrange housing for these boat people. Unfortunately, they can't muster enough volunteers to handle the huge numbers.

What should the class, as president, do? Should they let the refugees land and enter the nation? Should they turn them away? Maybe they should establish a holding area to house the

Each student gets a Reference Book.

The class takes the role of President of the United States.

Refugee crisis

Public opinion is split.

What should they do?

The Computer as a Discussion Generator

uninvited immigrants until they figure out what to do with them. Those who live in the state wonder how much support the incumbent will receive in the primaries if the refugees are allowed to land and move into the main city. Members of the volunteer agencies, on the other hand, call on the President to lend a helping hand to these struggling visitors from another land.

The students use history as a guide.

This situation is not an unfamiliar one for the nation. Throughout its history the United States has dealt with waves of immigrants, welcome and unwelcome, approaching its shores. And the country has responded in different ways with varying repercussions. Those past experiences provide valuable insight for the students as they progress through the simulation. Before making any decisions, however, the group must determine its goals. That's the first thing that the computer asks for. What are the group's priorities?

Setting priorities

Four goals, which are described in more detail in the Reference Book, are listed on the screen: Win local support for the primary election; Hold down costs to the government; Improve your national reputation as a good President; Improve life for the refugees. The computer wants to know which one the group feels is the most important. I like to have the students develop their own personal sets of priorities before initiating a class discussion. That way they're already invested in some point of view. It's interesting to hear how kids perceive these issues, and reaching a consensus can take some time. What's more important: helping the refugees or winning reelection? Opinions can vary widely, but few groups make holding down costs a high priority. Of course, as teacher you can sway the group in any direction you like. The program makes playing devil's advocate easy. With one class of fifth graders, I introduced the notion of federal deficit. Did they have any idea of the size of the national debt? $100? $1000? When I had finished adding the zeroes to one trillion dollars, the class was convinced that limiting spending should be the number one goal. Naturally, I then reminded them of the poor, suffering refugees, risking their lives for a taste of freedom in the United States. The poor kids were so confused it was great. They were beginning to truly appreciate the types of complex dilemmas

I play devil's advocate.

The Computer as a Discussion Generator

and trade-offs politicians face daily.

After all, that's the point. These decisions shouldn't be as simple as "nuke 'em." And four, in this case, "White House Advisors" (see the sample Reference Book page on the right) constantly reappear to offer conflicting bits of advice and direction to further complicate matters. Their faces are displayed on the screen at every decision-point. The terms under their faces point to paragraphs listed alphabetically in the reference books. (The content of those paragraphs could have been available on the screen, but then the students couldn't take them home to read and study.) The first set of advisor references in the Immigration simulation are: Explainer, Protectionist, Liberty Statue, and Trade-offs. Again, depending on time, I'll break the class up into four groups — one for each advisor — and have them read and prepare summaries of the advice offered. Then I'll ask a representative from each group to make a presentation to the rest of the class. For this first decision, the advisors introduce themselves and explain their overall points of view. The explainer tells the group that his job is to explain anything that isn't clear about the available choices. Letting the refugees in, he elaborates, would basically just set them loose in the city. A naval barricade would be used to turn them away if that were the option selected, and some nearby abandoned army barracks could be used for the holding area choice. The Protection-

---

Before you decide...

Before you begin considering what course of action you will follow, take a moment to think about what you hope to accomplish. In your position as the President you have four goals which are listed below. (The goals are described in more detail on the next page.) Which of the goals is the most important to you? Which is the least important? Think about your goals and then rank them in order from most to least important. How well you do in this situation depends on your priorities. Accomplishing your highest priority is worth more points than achieving those you feel have less value.

Your Goals
A) Win local support for the primary election.
B) Hold down costs to the government.
C) Improve your national reputation as a good leader.
D) Improve life for the refugees.

Your White House Advisors

You have four White House Advisors, experts in the field, to help you make informed decisions. During each turn, they will point you to references which are listed alphabetically in this book. Look up and read what they have to say. The opinions they have to offer can be helpful, but you don't have to agree with them. Here's what your advisors have to say about your current situation:

#1 EXPLAINER   #2 PROTECTIONIST

#3 LIBERTY STATUE   #4 TRADEOFFS

The advisors offer conflicting suggestions...

77

...each supported by historical analogies and persuasive arguments.

ist, as you can predict, wants to turn the refugees away. She says we have our own citizens to take care of first and that the nation is too crowded to accept all comers. In fact, she cites rising population density figures to support her arguments. The Liberty Statue advisor reminds the group of American idealism embodied in the words of Emma Lazarus, "Give me your tired, your poor..." We can't turn our backs on these people. The fourth advisor raises questions. America's cultural diversity, she claims, is part of what makes this country great. But, at some point, as more and more people flock to our shores, do we begin to give up some of the ways of life we love? She doesn't know what we should do. Turning them away seems very cruel, but so does putting them in a holding area. She wonders if the government has the right to lock these people away.

Using the past to enlighten the present.

The advisors serve a number of purposes. They present points of view the students may not recognize on their own. They point to historical analogies to remind the class that the past can enlighten the present. They arm kids, who might not otherwise express themselves, with well-formed arguments, giving them support for their opinions. The discussions can be very dynamic, and I often find myself in the position of struggling to find a way to resolve an exciting debate. It's a nice position to be in. Normally, I'll turn to the democratic process and hold a vote.

Students must face the consequences of their decisions.

Each decision has its consequences demanding further action by the students, guided by more references from the advisors. Should the group devise ways to evaluate the refugees? Should they offer government support to help the newcomers assimilate into the society? What about the continual flow of illegal immigrants from that region of the world? How will they respond to media criticism of their actions? Depending on their choices, the group could face a variety of consequential situations. The five decisions they will make could lead them down any one of over 300 possible paths. There are no right or wrong answers, and the same decision won't necessarily result in the same outcome. The students have no guarantee that a particular policy will always be effective.

The Computer as a Discussion Generator

Decisions, Decisions is a great tool for sparking student to student interaction. The computer may drive the discussion, but it is not the center of attention, the kids and their ideas are. The process works well in many areas and at many different levels, not just with the "good" kids, as many teachers I've encountered assume. Here's what one teacher wrote to the designers after using one of the titles in a setting very different from the one I've described:

Discussions aren't just for the "good kids."

As I turned the computer on, my students waited to see color and magic light up the screen. How delighted they were to find that all the color and magic came from them and their ideas! We were in motion, and travelled from student to student, to chalkboard, to dictionary, to computer. The group consisted of eight emotionally disturbed 12-15 yr. olds with some very distorted concepts and self-centered views of the world. I had so much to teach and learned even more! Fortunately for my small group, we had this experience.

"...all the color and magic came from them and their ideas."

I sincerely appreciate the amount of thought and energy that went into your designs. Several ideas were sparked on how to adapt the *Decisions* concept to many of the social concerns relevant to a special needs teen population...

S.M.A.R.T. Choices

The ability of the computer to generate positive talk about sensitive issues among even "special" groups is best exemplified by a variation of the *Decisions, Decisions* approach found in *S.M.A.R.T. Choices*. The S.M.A.R.T. stands for Students Master the Art of Responsible Thinking, and the package targets the growing at-risk population in school.

The opening situation here involves drugs and a friend in school. As students progress through the simulation, issues of peer pressure, self-esteem, and substance abuse all arise. Advisors, cartoons, and built-in role playing exercises force the group to consider each decision from several points of view and with appropriate information. In what can become a highly

Decision-making for at-risk students

79

The Computer as a Discussion Generator

Discussing sensitive issues that all students must face

Role playing simulations for young kids

The computer as campfire

Dealing with the "new kid" in school

sensitive discussion where teacher intervention must be carefully charted, the Random Student Picker emerges here as a particularly valuable management asset.

Despite its focus, *S.M.A.R.T. Choices* is not limited to at-risk students. Substance abuse and its root causes affect kids at all levels and abilities, but not all classroom teachers are prepared to open up discussions about these issues. The package, with its reference books and support activities, is best used under the supervision of experienced professionals as part of a broader substance abuse program. Getting students to discuss constructively while developing decision-making skills will not by itself resolve at-risk problems in the school, but it's an awfully good start.

Choices, Choices

Another series, based on *Decisions, Decisions*, is available for the early elementary grades: *Choices, Choices*. Running closer to the content of *S.M.A.R.T. Choices*, these role playing simulations concentrate on the kinds of personal decisions and issues young children face everyday — peer pressure, honesty, responsibility, and so on. They are set in recognizable contexts, from the playground to the classroom. Each one strives to help students develop the decision-making skills they can use today and build on for tomorrow. The programs' use of pictures and graphics, along with the centrality of the teacher, make them accessible even to preliterate children.

As with the *Decisions* series, *Choices* requires only one computer in the classroom, but I would resist using a large display device. I prefer to have small kids, when possible, gather around the machine, either pulling up chairs or sitting on the floor. Someone suggested the metaphor "computer as campfire." It's corny, but I like it. It conjures the right kind of warm feeling of shared experiences and storytelling.

At the beginning of the program, the software displays a little captioned video strip that summarizes the situation. In *On the Playground*, for example, the class takes the role of a girl at recess. She has brought her special ball with her in preparation for playing her favorite game with her best friends. As they prepare to play, however, they notice a new kid standing nearby.

He looks different — he's got a triangle head — and he looks like he wants to play. Should she invite him to join them? Or should she ignore him? How will her friends get along with him? As in *Decisions*, the students must first examine their goals. What's more important: helping the new kid make friends or having fun during recess? What about staying out of trouble?

Drawings of the goals and of the possible outcomes from the available choices help the students think through their actions and begin to predict the consequences of their decisions. The discussions can be very revealing, and the teacher's guide suggests a number of activities for follow-up and to support the transfer of the emerging process for decision-making. The digressions into the real life experiences of your students can lead to some immediate and valuable interventions.

In fact, *Choices, Choices*, *S.M.A.R.T. Choices*, and *Decisions, Decisions* all encourage interesting peripheral discussions without the usual cost of such movements from the topic at hand. Kids, as I'm sure you know, are experts at changing the subject. You're in the middle of a discussion or presentation and you spot a hand sort of half-raised near the back of the room. "Yes, Kristen," you nod. "Oh, never mind. It's a stupid question," she demurs. "There's no such thing as a stupid question," you prompt, repeating some foolishness you heard as a student yourself. "Are those new shoes?" "Why yes, they are new..." And the next thing you know, you're spending twenty minutes talking about your wardrobe. Now, not all digressions travel so far from the main discussion. However, even a brief foray into student attitudes about politicians in the midst of a

Kids are experts at changing the subject.

"Mr. Dockterman, are those new shoes?"

interesting digressions without the risk of getting lost

debate about immigration or a retelling of someone's personal experiences as a new kid in a school arising from an examination of peer pressure can leave you at least temporarily lost. "That was a very interesting sidelight. Now, where were we?" This is a great feature of *Decisions* and *Choices* – they are excellent place keepers. You can take your class on an enlightening excursion into a related topic secure in the knowledge that the computer will be waiting for you when you return. You can pick right up where you left off, continuing to delve deeper and deeper into the issues you're considering.

an exhilarating experience

In summary, the software described here serves two purposes. First, it helps you create a compelling context that drives students to acquire, explore, and discuss relevant content and behavior. Second, it helps you manage that exploration and discussion. It is an exhilarating experience for both you and your students.

The Computer and Cooperative Learning

It's not surprising that cooperative learning has become a popular theme in current educational discussions. There is something very special about kids working in teams, cooperating, collaborating, creating and sharing an enthusiasm for learning. It's especially exciting when the teams are interacting with each other as well. As a high school student, I loved being a member of the British delegation at Yalta, plotting strategies to confound our classmates in their roles as Stalin and Roosevelt. Or from elementary school, I have fond memories of contributing to the whale project or to the classroom store. These activities happened rarely, but they are moments I may never forget.

Cooperative learning is a hot topic.

As a teacher, I wanted to recreate those moments in my own classroom. I craved them, but I was also scared about trying to arrange them. Small group activities seem so potentially disruptive. They're not like independent projects where kids are supposed to be working quietly on their own. Nor are they like whole group discussions where you maintain control of the action. These multi-group simulations demand simultaneous events. You just can't be everywhere at once. Potential discipline crises made my colleagues nervous and me anxious. What if things got out of hand? How could I possibly manage several small groups at once successfully? How could I insure that each member of each group remained involved? Despite the obstacles I attempted these activities, not as often as I would have liked and not without great exhaustion, but I gave them a shot.

Small group activities can be scary.

You probably knew that I was going to come to this point sooner or later, but, believe it or not, a single computer in your classroom can help you foster cooperative learning. With the right software, the machine can reinforce a healthy division of

The computer can help.

The Computer and Cooperative Learning

Most learning in school is competitive.

Cooperative learning versus learning in groups

The expert system

***Inter*dependence is the goal.**

labor that gets your students interacting with each other as it paces a number of groups through an activity. But before I offer some examples of how this process works, I'd like to devote a little more time describing why it's worth the effort.

What is cooperative learning anyway?

The notion of kids working together in groups is not new. Most activities that occur on the playground are group-oriented, and most classrooms are organized around groups, usually large ones. Group learning, however, is not necessarily synonymous with cooperative learning. After all, the bulk of school activities are competitive, not cooperative. The class may be taught as a group, but the participants, the students, often compete with one another for grades or other academic rewards.

Even most small group activities that traditionally take place in the classroom are not really cooperative. The turn-taking that occurs when students are forced to share a limited resource, like a computer or a book, involves a degree of cooperation, although a better term might be agreement. The kids agree to abide by the rules of sharing, but the actual activity is focused on the individual.

The same is true of small group, expert activities. You know the kind. A team of four students is given the task of preparing a report on Egypt, and each student becomes an expert. One kid builds a model pyramid, a second writes a report about religion and daily life, a third charts the progression of pharaohs and dynasties, and the fourth prepares a menu of ancient Egyptian delicacies for the rest of the class to sample. Their results are pooled into a final presentation. Now the pooling process might be somewhat cooperative, but the bulk of the effort is done independently.

The key to cooperative learning is *inter*dependence. The members of the group must interactively need each other and have a stake in each one's understanding and success. Creating this type of cooperative environment in your classroom is not at all easy, and it is something with which few teachers (and few students) have had any experience.

Even some of the "cooperative learning" techniques offered

by its supporters can easily dissolve when both teachers and students are confused about their roles. For example, a beginning cooperative learning strategy is to divide your class into small groups of four students each. Each member of the group should take a number from 1 to 4. Assign some questions to the class (whatever is appropriate for what you're teaching). Then randomly pick a number from 1 to 4, and that person from each group will be the one to present the answer to the question. Everyone in the group gets the same grade. In essence, this organization creates an incentive for the group to make sure that every one of its members knows the answers to the questions. They are forced to share ideas and information. It sounds cooperative. Interdependency, however, can quickly shift to dependency if, as so often happens in group work, the "smart" kid does all the work and then simply gives the answers to his or her teammates. That's how it worked in my junior high math class. The teacher had divided us into teams of 4 students. Whenever we received assignments, my three partners usually just watched me go to work. When I finished, they copied the answers. Cooperative learning at work.

Interdependence can easily become dependence.

Kids need to learn how to work together.

For many of these techniques to work, the kids must be prepared and willing to accept a variety of leadership and facilitator roles. Not surprisingly, they need to be liberated from some rather restrictive patterns of traditional schooling.

Of course, before you attempt to transform your classroom into one that supports cooperative learning, you should be convinced that it is worthwhile. I think it is.

Why is cooperative learning important?

As an end in itself, cooperative learning has value in the curriculum. After all, teamwork and the ability to communicate successfully and constructively are essential parts of the social world in which we live and work. Recent research by folks like Robert Slavin at Johns Hopkins, Spencer Kagan at the University of California, and David and Richard Johnson at the University of Minnesota, however, suggests that cooperative learning does much more than teach students how to work in groups. The *process* of learning cooperatively actually improves the acquisition and retention of content and skills

Students learn better cooperatively.

The Computer and Cooperative Learning

Learner as teacher; teacher as learner

One computer can help manage cooperative learning activities.

Geographic illiteracy

throughout the curriculum. In short, kids may learn better when they learn cooperatively.

That shouldn't be surprising. When you are forced to articulate your ideas and knowledge to another person or group, you have to process the information in a new way. Think about your own experiences as a teacher preparing to teach material new to you. You not only have to learn the material yourself, you must strive to understand how others will learn it as well. You organize and reorganize to an extent well beyond what you would do as an independent learner. This process can be a very potent learning mechanism.

This doesn't mean that all instruction should take the form of cooperative learning. It does suggest, though, that teachers should work to add cooperative learning strategies to their array of classroom teaching methods and strive to apply those strategies appropriately as they proceed through their curricula. And in fact, the computer can help in this effort.

Here are some examples:

World and U.S. Geography

You may find this hard to believe (although I doubt you will), but when I was teaching United States geography as part of a world cultures class (we called it "world cultures" to lull the kids into the false belief that there'd be no more states and capitals), my students were just not that interested. Jefferson City, Missouri. Concord, New Hampshire. Phoenix, Arizona. They just didn't care. For many of my Connecticut charges, the area between Pennsylvania and California could just as well not have existed. This geographic illiteracy is common across the country and among all ages. Can you find Utah on an outline map of the U.S.? Or can you name the leading corn producers in the country? (I hope I'm not embarrassing you.) Ignorance of international geography is even worse.

I'm not sure how much I blame people for their locational ignorance. After all, being handed a map with directions to memorize it isn't the most inspiring lesson plan imaginable. At the same time, the rolling hills of South Dakota or parched land of Ethiopia, as chunks of curricular content by themselves, generally don't inspire a passion for learning among students.

The Computer and Cooperative Learning

I was constantly seeking activities to make learning the location and general characteristics of the states and nations more fun, that would place these locations in a context more relevant than rote memorization. We played games, took trips, packed imaginary suitcases. (I drew the line at blowing up New Jersey.) Two more packages to add to that list of inspiring geography activities are themselves called *National Inspirer* and *International Inspirer*.

I've used each of these programs, which require only one computer, with as many as 35 people at once. They work very much the same way. I place the machine in a convenient corner of the room, in an accessible spot where five to seven students could easily gather (or maybe squeeze) around. I then divide the class into up to five teams (six teams for *International Inspirer*) with as many as seven players each. The ideal arrangement probably calls for fewer teams with fewer players, but, unfortunately, the ideal is rarely available in the schools. In any case, one member of each team receives a planning chart, to record the group's decisions, and the remainder of each team divides up a set of six U.S. maps for the national game and a set of four world map reference books in the international version. Each reference material displays different information about geographic, demographic, political, or historical characteristics of the area being studied (see sample map). Thus, on any given team, one player in *International Inspirer* would have a map book highlighting traits like population growth, eating habits, and occupational trends, while a second managed a set of maps displaying political affiliations, military spending, and refugee populations. A third student would master economic maps and a fourth general data (displayed in graphs) on all the nations. The main point is that every member of each team is responsible for different, but essential, data. Only together do they have all the information they need.

Now, here's how the game works. Once you've typed into the computer the number of teams, the machine will display starting information for you to read to each group. For instance, it might say that Team 1 is starting in Tanzania and looking for leading oil producers and members of NATO, gaining special bonus points for ending their round in a highly urbanized

One computer and 35 people – it can work.

Each team member gets different information.

Members of the group need each other.

country. Team 2 could be placed in Canada, looking for agricultural nations and leading energy consumers, with a special bonus awarded for ending up in a highly literate country. Each team would receive similar assignments.

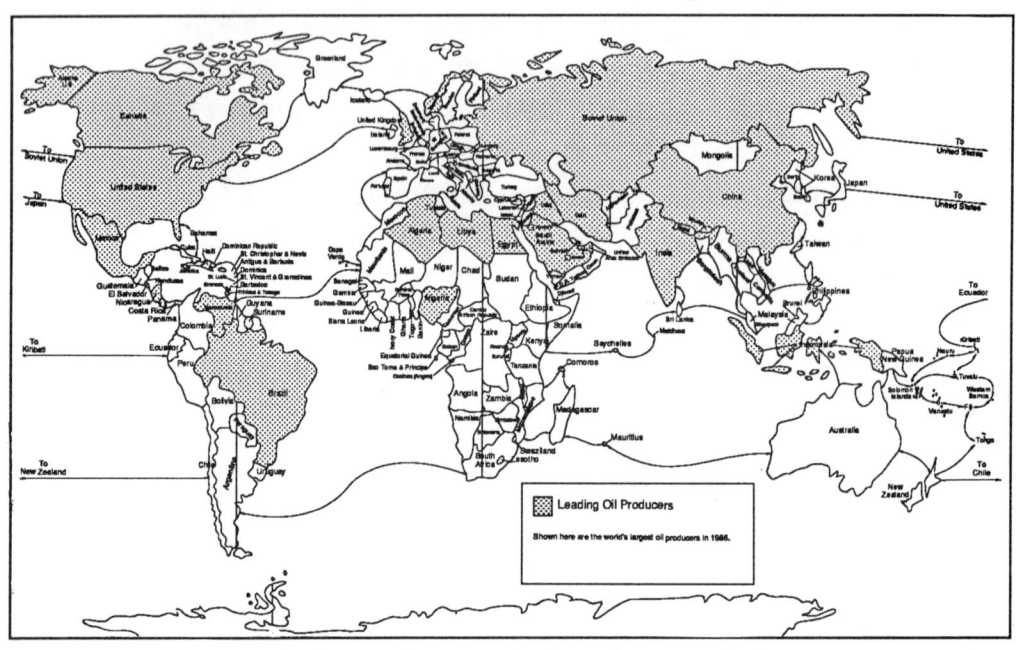

No doubt you're wondering what the kids are supposed to do with this information. Let's take Team 1. From Tanzania, they have up to ten moves — a move is a step to a bordering nation (there are special connections to move you across oceans and seas) — to visit as many major oil producers and NATO members as they can. The more nations from those categories that they visit, the more points they will receive. In addition, the group will receive bonus points if they end up, at their tenth move, in a country that has their particular bonus requirement for this turn — a highly urbanized nation. All the planning for the turn must be done at their seats in the group (see the sample turn sheet on the following page). Remember, someone on the team has information about oil, someone about NATO, someone about urbanization, and all about the best path to maximize points. When they're ready, the team members will go to the computer, type in their moves, await the results, and then receive their next assignment.

Like most small group activities, your classroom may take a turn toward the chaotic. Students will be arguing about whether to extend their path to Libya or leave themselves well-

"What countries are big oil producers?"

"Which are members of NATO?"

ROUND 1	ROUND 2	ROUND 3
Starting country: Tanzania	**Starting country:**	**Starting country:**
Looking for: Major Oil Producers	**Looking for:**	**Looking for:**
Looking for: Members of Nato	**Looking for:**	**Looking for:**
1 Kenya	1	1
2 Sudan	2	2
3 Egypt	3	3
4 Libya	4	4
5 Algeria	5	5
6 Morocco	6	6
7 Spain	7	7
8 France	8	8
9 Italy	9	9
End in a country with: High Urbanization	**End in a country with:**	**End in a country with:**
10 San Marino	10	10
Score this round: 280	**Score this round:**	**Score this round:**

situated in Turkey for the next turn. They may be boisterously correcting each other, "Just because a country has a big population doesn't mean it's densely populated!" Or you may hear them anxiously prodding their teammates for information, "Who has the map with cattle producers on it?" I know that some teachers find this kind of controlled chaos disconcerting. But I think it's worth it to get kids excited about something they need to know, not to mention the value of the cooperative learning experience.

Controlled chaos in the classroom

National Inspirer follows an almost identical procedure as students seek important resources like coal, oranges, and wheat matched to various topographical characteristics of the states. The editors at *inCider* (November, 1988) magazine

The Computer and Cooperative Learning

"...fostering both cooperative and competitive spirits."

Learning to be a leader and a follower

Little Shoppers Kit helps kids manage a store.

summed up the power of this U.S. geography package very nicely. They played the game in their office with teams of players like you'd have in the classroom. By the way, that effort to simulate the group experience, even just in reviewing the product, is an important part of evaluating software designed for this environment. It's very difficult to get the true flavor of a multi-group activity when you play it by yourself. The *inCider* conclusion: "This educational game creates a competitive furor that makes searching the states for the nation's leading producers of beef or cotton — or any of thirteen other natural resources — as exciting as discovering the Grand Canyon. It *inspires* learning, as well as fostering both cooperative and competitive spirits."

Cooperative Learning for Beginners

The kind of social interplay that takes place in programs like *National* and *International Inspirer* is wonderful for students; it may also be unusual for them. The traditional competitive environment of the school does not prepare kids for cooperative learning experiences where they must be willing to accept a variety of leadership and facilitator roles within their groups. When should I be assertive? When patient and passive? How do I make sure everyone's ideas are heard? How do I make sure that I am heard?

The social skills that make cooperative learning work (along with a healthy competitive drive) should be fostered when students are young and continued throughout their academic lives. Some of this growth already happens on the playground, but it is often haphazard and undirected. Existing roles tend to be reinforced rather than challenged; leaders remain leaders and followers stay followers. Structured experiences that place students in different positions and promote sensitivities to other points of view can provide a valuable underpinning for later cooperative activities. One elementary school package that helps create such as experience in a real world context is called *Little Shoppers Kit*.

This package (I hesitate to call it software because it comes with so much stuff) includes everything you need, from nifty ideas to plastic grocery store items, to open a little store in your

The Computer and Cooperative Learning

2nd grade classroom. The software portion of the *Little Shoppers Kit* was designed by two marvelous elementary school teachers as an aid for doing math at the cash register and as a group management tool. It is the latter usage that is of particular interest here and is best understood in the context of a day at the store.

Picture the classroom in your mind. Desks are arranged in groups around the room. The computer and printer sit on a cart in the corner next to two desks pushed together to form a long table. The teacher, having booted the software, announces that it's time to do stores. One group of four students moves toward the computer. Most of the rest get busy preparing shopping lists. We will concentrate on the small group. One member of the group, the manager, presses Return to open the store. She sees a list of roles and duties that looks something like this:

One students takes the role of the store manager.

```
STOCK CLERK
☐ Place items on shelves.
☐ Be sure stock is in place.
CASHIER
☐ Get money for cash drawer.
☐ Sort cash drawer money.
BAGGER
☐ Put bags in place.
☐ Clear off counter.
```

The teacher can set the roles and duties to match the situation.

As the other members of the group, who are playing the different roles, report that each task is complete, the manager checks it off on the computer. When all is ready, the manager can open the store to the public (or at least to the rest of the class).

At this point, the computer turns into a sort of smart cash register that adds up items (using preset codes, like the UPC stickers in real stores), prints out receipts, and helps the cashier make the correct change with a smart place-value change maker. The students stay in their roles, and if problems arise the manager is called in. It is his or her job to keep the store running smoothly, to make sure that everyone in the group is doing his or her job.

The computer turns into a smart cash register.

Students have more jobs at closing time.

Rotating jobs gives students experiences in different roles.

The computer can make what you like to do easier.

Facing the deficit

When it's time to close the store (a timer can be set to control how long the store stays open) a buzzer sounds. The computer calls the manager back to a new check list of duties for cleaning up and shutting down the store. The group takes a final tally and calls the next shift for its turn. A new group of students replaces this work crew. (Let me note here that a convenient built-in editor lets you create just about any kind of store or cafe or doughnut shop you like.)

Now I may not have thought to add this program to the section on cooperative learning if I hadn't seen it being used by a wonderful teacher. She took a lot of time helping students succeed in their roles, be it manager or bagger. And she made sure to rotate students through the different jobs so everyone had a chance to be both leader and follower. I'll never forget how she gently prodded one manager to take charge while silently holding back an aggressive cashier. *Little Shoppers Kit* created an ideal, life-like situation for exploring roles and relationships. (Remember how life skills appeared on the list of educational goals?)

You may wonder, as I did, whether or not such a fantastic teacher needed this program. Maybe not. She had been doing stores and developing social skills for many years without the computer. But the machine did help. It made the whole process easier. This is a statement worth repeating: the computer doesn't have to revolutionize your classroom or education in general to be a valuable tool. There's nothing wrong with making it easier to do the things we like to do.

The Budget Crunch

The newspapers have been filled with headlines about the federal deficit and the national debt, but how many people know what they mean? Is it bad to be in debt? Should the government be profitable? On what does it spend the money? How can and does it generate revenues? These questions face not just national leaders, but local ones as well. Communities across the country, large and small, regularly confront the trade-offs between fiscal restraint and the call for public services. How do we teach our students about these crucial, everyday issues?

The most direct response to the last question is simply to

teach our kids directly through lecture and presentation. Let's explain the situation to them. But if adults, despite daily elaborations in the papers and on the news, struggle to comprehend the complexities of these issues, how can we expect our children to grasp them through abstract description? We should have them attend town and city council meetings and encourage their involvement in civic affairs. Let them see real people grappling with these trade-offs in a context that is familiar and accessible. However, as teachable moments — opportunities for explanation and elucidation — come and go in these real-life settings, we, as teachers, cannot always be present to exploit them. Wouldn't it be great if you could take your class to a heated budget meeting at city hall and be able to interrupt the action at any time to answer students' questions? To go one step further, wouldn't it be even better to have the kids actively participating in such a gathering, under your guidance and control?

Experience can be the best teacher.

Classroom simulations of real world adventures, whether court room dramas, dangerous sea voyages, or town meetings, can be daunting for even the bravest of teachers. Yet the experiences can last a lifetime for students. *Our Town Meeting* is a multi-group software package that helps you simulate a community gathering where town leaders struggle with financial and public service issues. It assists you in establishing a context in which the concepts of debt and debt management can come alive for students.

Simulations offer controlled experiences.

Our Town Meeting is designed, ideally, for a group of 15 or fewer students to be divided into 3 smaller teams or agencies. Unfortunately, class sizes in this country rarely come as small as 15, not that they shouldn't. Nonetheless, *Our Town Meeting* remains an interesting example of another way a single computer can promote and manage multi-group activities.

Our Town Meeting

An introductory sequence in the program presents the following scenario: Your town is the least popular in the country (actually it ranks eighth out of the ten in this fictional world). The job of the class is to reach the number one ranking within ten years. Unfortunately, the town, like many in the nation, has no money. It can, however, borrow money to pay for projects that will generate revenues and improve the town's image. The

The Computer and Cooperative Learning

You, as mayor, run the town meeting.

students, divided into 3 agencies of four to five kids each, take the job of researching and proposing these projects. You play mayor, setting the budget and arbitrating discussions.

At the beginning of each turn (each turn is a year), you first determine how much money your students should be allowed to spend for the year. In this simplified world, you can go up to three hundred dollars in debt over the course of the game. If you exceed that limit, the bank forecloses and the game is over. (While the $300 amount allows kids to focus more on the issues than the computation, the numbers clearly do not match the real world. Relative values are accurate, but, as part of the simulation debriefing — something you should do with any simulation, computer-based or otherwise — be sure to examine true costs for municipal projects.) While you're setting the budget, each group will be selecting a project from the catalog (see example on left) to research at the computer. The small group decision-making is a microcosm of the larger town meeting to follow. Individuals lobby for their favorite choices, preparing logical and emotional arguments for why their group should propose an amusement park or pro team.

The software calls each agency to the computer one at a time and asks them to indicate their project selection for the year. All members of the group gather around the machine. Three graphs appear on the screen, which is divided into separate sections. One graph displays the results of a survey on the project's

---

Project Catalog

AGENCIES - Proposed: several additional agencies to help oversee the running of the town. It has not yet been decided exactly what those agencies would do.

AIRPORT - Proposed: a small private and commercial airport at the edge of the town.

AMUSEMENT PARK - Proposed: a small amusement park on old Route 1.

BENCHES - Proposed: benches to line the streets in the downtown area.

BIKE PATH - Proposed: a series of bike paths on the west side of town.

BUS SYSTEM - Proposed: a commuter bus system for the downtown area.

CASINO - Proposed: a gambling casino outside of the downtown area.

CEMETERY - Proposed: a ten acre grass plot cemetery.

CONVENTION CENTER - Proposed: a convention center for business and town events.

DOWNTOWN - Proposed: a major redevelopment of the downtown area.

DUMP - Proposed: an area outside of town reserved for dumping the town's refuse.

FARBUSH - Proposed: a statue of ex-mayor Farbush to be placed in front of the town hall (proposed by ex-mayor Farbush.)

FERRY - Proposed: a ferry service to the town on the other side of the river.

FIRE DEPARTMENT - Proposed: a modernized fire department.

FREEWAY - Proposed: a conversion of old Route 1 to a freeway.

GARAGE - Proposed: a multilevel parking garage on Jefferson Ave.

GOVERNMENT BLDG. - Proposed: a new town hall.

HAZARDOUS WASTE SITE - Proposed: a site outside of town to permanently store hazardous waste.

HISTORICAL AREA - Proposed: a redevelopment of the old section of the town.

HOSPITAL - Proposed: a small modern public hospital.

INDUSTRIAL PARK - Proposed: an industrial park to accommodate light industry.

JAIL - Proposed: a secure building to house local criminals.

LIGHTS - Proposed: high intensity street lights for the downtown area.

LOTTERY - Proposed: a daily dollar lottery for all residents of the town.

MALL - Proposed: a tasteful commercial mall on Jefferson Ave.

METERS - Proposed: parking meters for the congested streets in the downtown area.

MORE POLICE - Proposed: an increased number of uniformed police to patrol our streets.

NEW HOMES - Proposed: a fund to help townspeople to build homes.

NUKE PLANT - Proposed: a low wattage nuclear power plant to supply electricity to the town.

PARK - Proposed: conversion of a section of Thompson Forest to an official town park.

PLUMBING - Proposed: modernization of all of the old lead plumbing in town.

POLLUTION FORCE - Proposed: a pollution task force to monitor industry and automobiles in town.

PRO TEAM - Proposed: a professional baseball team to represent our town.

PUBLIC LIBRARY - Proposed: a public library for readers of all ages.

RESERVOIR - Proposed: conversion of Morse's pond to a reservoir for drinking water.

ROAD PAVING - Proposed: repaving of the Old Mill road.

SANITATION SERVICE - Proposed: a garbage pickup service for all residents.

SCHOOL - Proposed: a kindergarten through 12th grade school to replace the scattered and failing schools currently in town.

SEWERS - Proposed: improvement of the currently overloaded sewer system.

SPOTLIGHTS - Proposed: a set of spotlights to shine at the proposed site for the statue of Mayor Farbush.

STADIUM - Proposed: a stadium for large outdoor sporting events.

SWIMMING AREA - Proposed: a swimming area at the edge of Thompson Forest.

THEATERS - Proposed: rennovation of several of the old theaters in town.

TOLL ROAD - Proposed: conversion of Route 7 into a toll road to help raise money for repairs and maintenance.

TRAFFIC LIGHTS - Proposed: installation of traffic lights in the downtown area.

UNIVERSITY - Proposed: an institution of higher learning.

VISITOR CENTER - Proposed: a visitor center to assist tourists.

WATERFRONT - Proposed: redevelopment of old fishing docks for commerce and fun.

ZOO - Proposed: a children's zoo at the end of the Old Mill Road.

popularity. Another graph shows an 8-year revenue projection, and a final one offers 5 estimations of the project's cost. The information remains on the screen only for a few moments (you can control the timing). By limiting access with this timer, the software forces the members of the group to share responsibilities. No one student can gather all the data in the short amount of time available, but if each member of the group deciphers a different graph, all the essential information can be recorded. After the graphs, the students see an option for a scaled-down version of the project. In an effort to establish a professional baseball team in the community, for example, the group can save money by staying away from big name players for the first few years. The group is then sent back to its station to share what they've learned and plan the presentation for the town meeting. While one group is planning, the others are researching.

Timed displays force students to delegate responsibilities.

When all the agencies have completed their proposals, the teacher, as mayor, can convene a town meeting. Each group is asked to present a project to the whole class. What project are they proposing? How much will it cost? How will it benefit the town? You can have a lot of fun with these presentations if you encourage creativity and fanfare. Fifth and sixth graders, in particular, will make posters and signs which support their pet proposals. Often, the total amount of money requested by the three agencies will exceed the amount budgeted for the year. That's when the real fun starts. Should one or more of the projects be only partially funded? Should they be delayed completely? What's the town's priority: revenues or popularity? The ensuing debate provides a number of opportunities for you to make connections to actual issues and referenda currently on your own town's agenda.

How should you spend your limited resources?

When the funding decisions are finally made, the computer will report the results of their first year and graph the financial situation. As the town charts its path into debt, the class must seek projects that generate revenues both to finance future proposals and to pay off the money that is owed. The situation in the fictional world of the simulation begins to mirror the one faced by our own national government. How can we pay for public services without increasing a debt that is growing

Students as debt managers

dangerously large? It's amazing that, given an appropriate context, even relatively young kids can confront and even surmount the turmoil of debt management.

The computer as a social tool in the classroom

Each of the packages described in this chapter employs a different strategy to reinforce a cooperative learning environment in the classroom. Many additional strategies exist as well. It is somehow ironic that a machine so highly touted for its purported ability to individualize instruction should turn out to be such a useful tool for managing group activities. A single computer really can play a significant role in establishing a powerful academic as well as social environment in your classroom.

The Computer as Actor

I'd like to conclude this series of chapters by returning to the opening metaphor of the classroom as stage on which a variety of dramas, comedies, and tragedies are played. You, your students, and the devices in your classroom — including the computer, the chalkboard, and the overhead projector — constitute the actors and the props in these enactments, each taking different roles as the action dictates. I like this metaphor because it puts the story, not the actors, first. All too often pressures to use the technology turn the classroom stage into a showcase for the computer. But you'd never create a lesson in order to use or highlight a filmstrip projector.

The classroom is your stage.

In each one of the applications described in the previous pages, the computer always takes a supporting role. Keep it that way. The computer will truly be a successful classroom tool when it becomes as natural for us to use as the chalkboard, a reflexive tool for teaching.

Interactive Video, Multimedia, & All that Jazz

As I sit here writing this chapter, I am surrounded by journal headlines extolling the praises of multimedia, videodiscs, and interactive video. A new wave of enthusiasm is sweeping the world of educational technology. I wonder if this current excitement is an extension of the computer revolution or a brand new and separate entity in and of itself. It's a bit difficult to sort through. Although the rhetoric sounds disturbingly familiar, the terms all have new meanings. I've had so many questions, let me share with you some of the answers.

A new wave of enthusiasm...

Understanding the Basic Terms

What is Multimedia?

I thought I knew the answer to this basic question. After all, I remember "multimedia" presentations in the 1960s and '70s. They usually involved more than one slide projector and some music or narration. I recall watching multimedia extravaganzas on immigration, race, and any number of high tech topics, like space flight. Each one had a title that began with "The Magic of..." and had a certain psychedelic feel to it. Somehow I don't think that any of those multimedia shows would fit today's definition of the term.

So what's different about contemporary multimedia? The basic notion is the same. Multimedia means more than one medium. It mixes print, audio, video, and whatever else is available. Today, that whatever else includes computers. Computers are important because they make the whole thing interactive. What exactly does that mean? Well, that was my next question.

What is Multimedia?

Interactive Video, Multimedia & All that Jazz

You have the option of exerting some control.

What is Interactive Video?

Traditionally, video experiences, like watching television at home or a film in class, are passive endeavors. You sit and view a presentation created by someone you don't know and will never meet. With interactive video, you might have the option of exerting some control either in the creation of the video or in the viewing itself.

At one end of the spectrum, new video technologies and computer software make it much easier to create your own original video productions. My wife and I do a primitive version of this at home with the video camera we bought when our son was born. Connecting the camera to our VCR, we edit the raw footage (how many drooling faces does grandma really need to see?), insert titles, and create the final tape. If we added a computer to the process we could create special graphics and new sound to weave into the video. So, with the help of a computer, original video can be produced in school without the expense of building a semi-professional editing suite.

Aside from creating your own footage, the technology allows you to reorganize existing material. As a teacher you could selectively show whatever parts of a film you wanted your students to view. And as a viewer, you could sift through visual materials in any order you wanted. To fully appreciate this aspect of interactive video, you have to understand another piece of the picture: videodisc.

What does Videodisc have to do with this stuff?

The videodisc is not really a new technology. Videodisc players have been around since 1980. The videodiscs themselves look like large, 2-sided compact audio discs. You slide one into a player, hit play, and it works just like a videotape inside a VCR. You get sound and pictures. You can fast forward and reverse direction.

The big difference between videotape and videodisc comes when you want to access a still picture or section of movie that doesn't follow sequentially what you are currently viewing. With a VCR, you hold down fast forward or rewind until you get close to the piece you want, then you go back and forth until you hit it exactly. With videodisc, each frame of video (and you can have as many as 54,000 video frames per side) has a distinct code, a unique location on the disc. All you have to do is indicate that code on the player, and you're there at that frame, almost instantaneously. And unlike VCRs, videodiscs allow you to stare at that single still frame for as long as you want. It's a beautiful picture. Or you can press play and watch a movie. In fact, short movie pieces can be separately designated on the disc in segments called chapters. If you want to see that nice video on ringworms, just play chapter 5. It will stop automatically at the end of the segment.

Accessing information is easy.

If you hook a videodisc up to a computer, you can review, reconfigure, and *save* any organization of the video segments you want. In other words, with the appropriate software you or your students can do visual research, having the computer search for relevant video clips or stills. You can then customize existing footage into your own personal movie and/or still frame presentations.

(By the way, efforts to bring the power of all these technologies — computer, videodisc, and full motion color display — under one roof is rapidly proceeding. Alternative storage devices, like CD-ROM, are being built directly into computers. And with the help of new software, the computer acts simultaneously as the control mechanism as well as the display device for the video stored on the CD. The technology is slightly different, but the goals remain pretty much the same.)

You or your students can do visual research.

What's the Big Deal?

On the surface, the capabilities of interactive video sound great, the potential enormous. But before we sell another cow for some more magic beans (to steal a line from Tom Snyder), let's take a closer look at why this new technology is such hot stuff. What follows are some of the key selling phrases for interactive video and some commentary about each.

"Students can view material in any order they want."

Here's the argument: Not all kids learn the same way. With interactive video (and interactive text), each student can select the order that best suits his or her learning style and interests.

Students can take control and guide their own learning.

The goal for students to guide their own learning doesn't come without risks.

A student, thus, doesn't have to learn about Martin Luther King from birth to assassination. He or she could start with the "I have a dream speech" and then move to related parts of his life in an order that made sense for that individual.

Sounds great. If only it were that easy. The goal for students to take control and guide their own learning is certainly welcome and desirable. However, it doesn't happen automatically nor does the process come without risks, especially when done with a whole class at once. I'll relate one story to illustrate: A teacher was working with a fourth grade class using the program *InnerBodyWorks Junior* (described in the chapter "The Computer as a Presentation Tool"). The Hypertour mode of the program allows you to cruise through the human body in any order you want. The teacher, wishing to encourage student control, asked the class where they wanted to go. One student quickly responded, "I want to go to the penis" (which he pronounced "pennis"). Unfortunately, that wasn't where the teacher, or this class of fourth graders, was prepared to go. Some areas of investigation just demand preparation, care, and informed guidance, whether attempted by a group or an individual. How does this need for this external guidance mesh with the desire for student independence? It's a tough balance.

As I think about that balance, I consider my 4 month old son. (I consider him a lot, and, well, didn't Piaget spend a lot of time with his kids too?) I certainly want him exploring the world in his own way and at his own pace. But I would never leave him alone until I felt confident that he could navigate through his immediate environment successfully and independently. I don't think I'm being overly protective here. Left solely to their own devices, students might wander down marvelous paths of knowledge, yet still miss some essential information. Or they might just flounder aimlessly for hours. Or, worse yet, they might get themselves in trouble. Insufficient information or misinterpreted data can be very dangerous. Simply put, creating a healthy, nurturing setting for self-exploration takes a lot of work, and merely buying the equipment won't do it.

"Teachers can create their own presentations, becoming curriculum builders."

As this statement implies, student-directed learning isn't the only kind of learning that happens in school. Teachers still teach. After all, teacher-directed instruction is an incredibly efficient way to insure that students receive the mandated or desired curriculum. Multimedia/interactive video/videodisc can help teachers present this information in dynamic, customized ways.

I'm all for it. With a multimedia workstation (or just a computer, monitor, and videodisc player), teachers can do everything I described in the chapter on the computer as a presentation tool and more. You can integrate real pictures and full motion video into your lectures, demonstrations, and group explorations. Being able to show actual cell division in a biology lesson of your own design (as opposed to the design of the film maker) is wonderfully empowering. And while this technology does not by itself turn you into a curriculum builder — many of you have been doing that for years — it does add a new dimension to what you create.

One of the biggest obstacles to this application of the technology is access, both to the hardware and the software. If computers alone were hard for you to get your hands on, imagine what it's like if you need even more expensive equipment. I've covered this access question before, but it just won't go away. Availability of materials and the time to use them are just not built into current school organization. Excellent use of these tools requires getting them into your hands and lives. And that is another important battle to be fought.

Access to software is a separate but related issue. By software here, I mean video, lots of it. It's true that there is a great deal of existing video footage in the world. However, not all of it is good (all you have to do is turn on TV to see that!), and not all of it is available to schools. Nonetheless, much can and is being "repurposed" (that means it was developed for some other reason) for educational use. In fact, tremendous amounts of existing 16mm educational films have already been transferred to videodisc. Unfortunately, this transfer won't improve the quality. Fortunately, it will allow you to be more selective.

Sidebar notes:
Multimedia
Interactive video
Videodisc

Add a new dimension to your teaching.

Accessability

Creating quality original video for education is incredibly expensive.

"students...have grown up on MTV."

"If it ain't on TV, it ain't worth learnin'."

Anyway, it's not the availability of existing video that's the most significant problem. It's the lack of good affordable new stuff that threatens to undermine this whole revolution. Creating quality, original video for education is incredibly expensive. Can the school market support it? Sure, you'll be able to purchase consumer videodiscs of popular movies and re-edited news shows and documentaries, not to mention existing bad and boring educational film and slide dumped onto this new format. You'll even find a few grant-funded original pieces. But what good will this relatively small collection (compared to books in a library) do when you're teaching about civilizations in Africa or about fractions? Until the industry discovers some major production breakthrough that makes the development of *quality,* original educational video affordable, even if you do get your hands on the hardware you may find its promise limited.

"Today's students are visual learners who have grown up on MTV."

I love this statement, and it may even be true. Certainly, kids spend an incredible amount of time watching TV and playing video games. And they spend far too little time reading books. Maybe we really have finally reached the video age. Of course, this visual age was proclaimed at least as early as the 1860s with the invention of the magic lantern. But maybe now it has truly arrived. And if it is true, the argument goes, we can no longer rely solely on print to educate our children. "The age of illustration is upon us, and illustrate we must if we hope to gain and hold the attention of young and old" (1890). If we want interested students, then we must use video because that is their medium.

Sorry, I don't buy it, at least not entirely. Yes, we should use multiple forms of media in the classroom, if only to expose our students critically to the multiple forms of information packaging they will encounter in life. However, just because this generation appears to be hooked on TV doesn't mean we should throw in the towel and join the party. Quite the contrary, it means we have to work extra hard to enliven once again the "less popular" media, like books and magazines.

Besides, any effort to compete with music videos and high tech special effects will inevitably lead to failure. Education will never win a head-on battle with the consumer world. The under-resourced world of schools can barely afford the price of admission. We need to turn to fundamental issues, not flash, to solve our educational problems.

> We need to turn to fundamental issues, not flash.

"With videodisc kids can become producers of knowledge, not just receivers of knowledge."

One of the most commonly hyped visions of educational videodisc depicts a student making an incredibly dynamic, visual report to the rest of the class. I remember doing something like that when I was in junior high. A classmate and I researched African-American athletes. Since we planned on making a multimedia presentation in class, we took a lot of Polaroids of action shots from *The Sporting News* and *Baseball Digest*. (We were definitely young boys growing up in the midwest.) We also compiled statistical charts from a variety of books. When it was time to make the presentation, we asked the teacher to wheel an opaque projector into the classroom. We then took turns narrating the text of our report and shoving pictures and books under the opaque lamp as visual support. As I recall, it was an excellent report that took advantage of cutting-edge technologies, clearly a cut above the usual drone. I'm sure we received a good grade.

I tell this story to highlight several points. First, it is valuable for students to be producers of knowledge and organizers of information, not merely passive receptors of teacher and textbook talk. This notion, however, isn't new. Students have long been encouraged to do independent research and reports that went beyond copying passages from the encyclopedia, which brings me to my second point. You don't *need* videodisc to turn students into knowledge producers. A good library can do the trick. However, (point three) students should learn that multiple media are available for both research and presentation of information. Consequently, it seems like a good idea to encourage students to create their own original multimedia presentations. Be aware, though, that videodisc makes these presentations at once easier and more difficult to do.

> "...kids can become producers of knowledge, not just receivers of knowledge."

A good library can do the trick.

The more elaborate you get, the more equipment you need.

It's easier because with a videodisc player connected to a computer, all the tools are at your fingertips. You can search for specific visual support; organize it in any order that suits your needs; and tie text to various pictures and segments of video. I'm sure our presentation on African-American athletes would have been even more polished if we had had access to a multimedia workstation like this, assuming of course that our library of video material had what we needed. I've already discussed the potential difficulty of limited visual resources. Students, of course, can easily overcome that shortage by ranging beyond the realm of videodisc, which you really want them doing anyway. The more significant problem is the same one that plagues teacher-created presentations: access to the hardware. You aren't likely to have thirty available multimedia workstations sitting around your school. If you, the teacher, have trouble gaining access to the machinery, how are the thirty students in your class going to manage? One of the great things about books is that you can afford a lot of them. And almost every person comes equipped with the necessary technology to read them. Not so with videodisc.

The lesson here is simple. The more elaborate you get, the more equipment you generally need. The more equipment required, the less accessible it is. Don't get me wrong, these are great tools; but we have to think carefully about their best practical use in schools. How can we make this stuff work well in your classroom? I've got a few ideas. I'll get to them after discussing one final hype.

"With interactive video we can move away from oppressive linear thinking."

One of the most asked questions I hear concerning videodisc technology is, "Is it interactive?" I have to admit I'm often unclear about what the questioners mean. They may not know themselves, but they've been convinced that it's important. Somehow, the computer revolution has glorified the term "interactive," and those products that have it are better than those products that don't. I guess it's basically a matter of choice. Interactive video allows the user to choose his or her viewing path. Linear video decides that path for you.

But I'm still confused. Hasn't someone also determined and severely limited my universe in the interactive world? And don't people have some control over how they watch linear movies? You can always start, stop, fast forward, and rewind. If you're not afraid of breaking the film, you can even employ these features with a 16mm film projector. I've done it myself, but, then again, I was on the A-V squad in junior high school. And besides, linear isn't all that bad. I certainly appreciate the way Arthur Schlesinger, Jr. organizes history for my consumption or the manner in which e.e. cummings lays out a poem. And I would never think to read a novel by James Michener or view a movie by Alfred Hitchcock in any order I wanted.

I don't mean to imply that user control and manipulation of information isn't important. It is. I just want to keep it in perspective. The highly organized, progressive lessons that you build as a teacher still have value. So does the organizational input of an expert in the field. In many ways, a good linear presentation can be incredibly interactive. It can make you think; it can fill you with emotion; it can spark dialog; it can even prompt action.

Of course, this use of the term interactivity differs greatly from how it is typically applied to technology. In the latter realm, interactivity refers to the very narrow relationship between user and machine. Interactive video allows you to reorganize information. However, a much more powerful and richer kind of interactivity occurs among people. An interactive classroom buzzes with contact and communication among students. In fact, if you built a scale of interactivity ranging from sitting by yourself to, say, making love (a very interactive experience), interactive video and interactive classrooms would rest far apart from one another. The level of interactivity that occurs just between two individuals who merely stare at one another is infinitely greater than the choices offered when you connect a videodisc to a computer.

So, why am I ranting about interactivity? Because, as interesting as interactive technology is, it doesn't hold a candle to dynamic human interactivity, and that's what I really want to talk about. How can this new video/computer revolution spark

Interactive video vs. Linear video

I would never think to watch an Alfred Hitchcock movie in any order I wanted.

It can make you think...

Interactive Video, Multimedia & All that Jazz

...a much more powerful and richer kind of interactivity occurs among people.

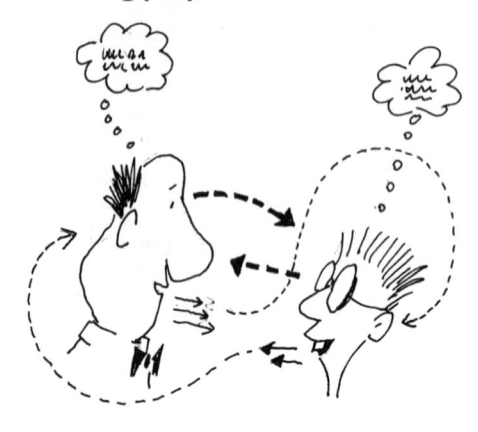

...it helps to create and enhance drama and pacing.

valuable person-to-person interactivity in a room full of students with one teacher and a limited amount of equipment? Let me share a couple of examples.

TalkVideo: Video for the Interactive Classroom

In the next section I am going to describe two products that integrate video technology into dynamic group activities for the classroom. Each product uses video in different ways. In one the video plays a familiar role to anyone who goes to movies or watches prime time TV: it helps to create and enhance drama and pacing. The pacing element is a key piece that separates linear video from linear print in its ability to draw audiences into a compelling context at a controlled pace. Individuals can't read ahead with video. Everybody watches the same thing at the same time. And when the video stops, each viewer is left at the same point. That, as you will see, can be a useful feature for group classroom activities. In the other package, the video is completely non-linear. Its role is not so much to pace as it is to provide rich context that would not otherwise be available. In both cases, however, the underlying process remains much the same. We call that process "TalkVideo." It's Tom's term, one that is meant to reflect an aspect of an existing medium: talk radio. You know the late-night call-in shows that incite dynamic discussion and emotion. TalkVideo has a similar goal — constructive talk in the classroom. But enough with general statements, on to the specific examples.

Talking About Math

I was a straight A student in math from elementary school right through high school. I was the odds-on favorite in any flashcard competition, and everyone wanted to be my partner in any "group" work. (Group work usually meant that my teammates waited for me to finish the problems, then copied the answers.) I remember my fifth grade teacher regularly urging me to "show my work." Although I never did, she had to concede, "You can't argue with success." And success in K-12 math, whether multiplication and division or calculus, meant getting the correct answer.

Riding this history of right answers, I entered upper level calculus as a freshman at Yale brimming with confidence. I had scored well on my AP's, and figured college math would continue to be "easy." WRONG! I was completely lost. Suddenly, math wasn't just about right answers. Being able to complete volumes of computations wasn't enough. I had to know what I was doing, and I had to be able to articulate it. There was a large gap in my math education, one that needn't have waited until college to be filled. In fact, it needed to be addressed early on. Students need to be able to go beyond filling in the final answer, they need to be able to describe how they got there.

Suddenly math wasn't just about right answers.

The Wonderful Problems of Fizz & Martina is a series of dramatic math videos that attempts to fill this gap, forcing upper elementary students to articulate the process of math problem solving. Here's how it works. Wheel a VCR and monitor into your classroom — that's all the high-tech equipment you'll need. Divide your class into small groups, making sure to maintain a good mix of ability levels and backgrounds in each team. Every team gets one of six different color cards and every student a workbook. The package comes with 30 workbooks along with a deck of duplicate color cards which you will use to randomly select teams.

The Wonderful Problems of Fizz & Martina

The video and workbooks operate in conjunction with one another. Some introductory exercises on the video show kids how the process works and prepare them for cooperative group work. For now let me dive into one of the adventures. You tell your students to get their pencils poised for note-taking, and you turn on the VCR. If you're watching the second episode on volume 2, you'll see Martina posing as Julie and waiting on Mr. and Mrs. Tweetwig at the restaurant. Julie, you see, is off with Fizz at the fire. Anyway, Martina explains that the dinner special is only $8 and very good. Students jot some notes in their workbooks. The Tweetwigs order 2 specials (more notes). During the course of the meal, Martina impresses not only the Tweetwigs, but Miss Angel Eyes as well. Could she help them with Project Sphinx? Mr. Tweetwig announces that he wants to give Martina a big tip, 50% of the cost of the 2 dinners (still more notes), but he only has $25 (one final jot). Does he have enough money to pay the bill and the tip?

The video stops. You can see that, like real life, there's a lot happening. Students are captured by the rich drama, but they have a problem to attack. In their small groups they sift through the information and set to work. The page in the workbook for this episode asks three questions. First, "How much will Mr. and Mrs. Tweetwig's total bill be?" Calculating this answer isn't usually the toughest challenge for the group, assuming they have all the correct information (and among the team members they almost always do). By the way, the answer to this problem is $24.

It's the second question that provides the most significant challenge for students, and, not surprisingly, it's the question that builds the most understanding of what they have just done. "Write, in a complete sentence (or two), how you figured out the answer to question 1. Do NOT use numbers in your explanation." The computation is trivial compared to the task of articulating that mathematical process in simple language. With this step, math becomes something more than mere number manipulation. It has to do with real life and concrete processes. Making this leap is an incredible effort for kids, but it is a worthwhile one. And they get better and better with practice.

The third question asks students to explain why the answer to the problem is important for Mr. and Mrs. Tweetwig. The final step demands that the group return to the original context. In life, math doesn't end with the numerical answer. The response to a problem has consequences; the drama continues. Such is the case with Fizz & Martina.

Students jot some notes in their workbooks.

The Acting — Practice Quiz 1

1. How much will Mr. and Mrs. Tweetwig's total bill be?
   24 dollars
   - dinner special $8
   - ordering 2 specials
   - 50% tip

   3 steps
   Addition 8+8=16
   Divide 2√16 = 8
   Addition 8+16=24

2. Write, in a complete sentence (or two), how you figured out the answer to question 1. Do NOT use numbers in your explanation.

   I added together the cost of 2 dinner specials then divided that amount in half to determine the tip and added that amount to the cost of the dinners.

3. — Compare 24 and 25 —
   Write, in a complete sentence (or two), why your answer to question 1 is important for Mr. and Mrs. Tweetwig. Use 25 in your answer.

   The dinner will cost 24 dollars and the Tweetwigs have 25 dollars, so they have enough with a dollar to spare!

Like real life, there's a lot happening.

Okay, the students working in their groups have completed the three questions, now what do you, the teacher, do? Remember those color cards I mentioned earlier? Each team has one. Well, shuffle the remaining cards and then turn the top one over. Whatever team matches the color on the card is the one responsible for answering the first question. Walk over to the group and pick up the workbook of someone on the team. I select individual students differently depending on my objective at the moment. If, for instance, the group has not been working well together, I might choose the team member who has been left out, because I can use this process to help get them involved. I hold the workbook in my hand and ask the student to tell me the answer. He or she must remember the response, not through memorization hopefully, but through understanding. If the student response is correct, both orally and in the workbook, then everyone on the team gets an award card (they're called "Budge" cards in the activity) that depicts one of the characters from the video. You can give these award cards any value you want, but don't worry, the students will give them more worth than you could ever assign.

Everyone on the team gets rewarded.

Some of the best dynamics occur, however, when the student's answer is wrong. In that case, no one on the team gets an award card. It's a standard cooperative learning technique used to diffuse responsibility. When the selected member of the group is right, the whole team wins. When the selected student is incorrect, the whole team loses. The important role for the teacher is constantly to reinforce the group over the individual. So when one team member is incorrect, it is *not* the single student who failed the group, it is the group that failed the student. So, in this case, you say to the student with the wrong answer, "Too bad your teammates let you down. I'm sure *they* won't let it happen again." It's amazing how quickly a group will then work to embrace its struggling members.

Math becomes something more than mere number manipulation.

It is not the single student who failed the group, it is the group that failed the student.

Anyway, you follow the same technique for each of the three questions. When all are answered, you press play, and the video continues. The answers are immediately integrated into the context of the story and new problems begin to emerge.

The video creates the setting, enhances the drama, and controls the pacing. *You* run the class, and it's a dynamic one.

Cooperative Exploration of Space

This second product may sound like ones mentioned in the chapter on the computer and cooperative learning. It has many of the features of, say, *National* or *International Inspirer*, *Our Town Meeting*, and *Decisions, Decisions*. But it has an important additional feature: real, actual, true-to-life video footage.

The Great Solar System Rescue

The Great Solar System Rescue was developed with the help of a grant from the federal Star Schools program for the improvement of middle school science. It could not have been developed otherwise. The source footage from NASA, the Jet Propulsion Lab, and other places was affordable enough. But editing video (and I mean editing and mixing in graphics and sound effects, not just reorganizing segments) for a dedicated educational experience is very costly. And shooting new, high quality, full motion video is enormously expensive. The school market is stretching to support this kind of development without outside help.

I want to emphasize this point from the outset. Despite new technologies, good educational film (as opposed to consumer video that happens to be slightly repurposed for schools) is still expensive to produce and hard to find. While I think that *The Great Solar System Rescue* is wonderful (of course I helped to design it), it is not typical. The educational industry cannot yet support this kind of production on its own. You may find wonderful nuggets out there, but you will likely struggle to fill the bulk of your curricular needs.

Enough with the disclaimers — how does the program work? First, you'll need a videodisc player. Second, you will need some way to tell the videodisc player what to play at any given time. *The Great Solar System Rescue* videodisc cannot simply be set to play and then viewed as a linear movie. There is nothing linear about it. It is not something to watch; it is a dynamic group experience. Depending on the choices students make in the activity, different video pieces will be displayed. You need some way to indicate which pieces. You have three choices: a remote control for the videodisc, a barcode reader, or a Macintosh computer. The first two options are relatively inexpensive and don't demand wheeling multiple pieces of equipment into your classroom. The computer option, however, offers additional classroom management features. If you've got the two connected, it's probably the way to go. I use whatever is available.

Once the equipment is arranged, it's time to arrange the classroom. Like *The Wonderful Problems of Fizz & Martina*, this program also asks that you organize your students into small cooperative groups. Four on a team is ideal. Each team consists of four experts — an astronomer, a geologist, a meteorologist, and an historian. Each expert receives a unique "expert" booklet and a worksheet for analyzing the information the class is about to see and hear.

Once you have organized the groups, just start the first mission. I love to really push the fiction. You see, due to some computer malfunction, several space probes have been lost in our solar system. It's the job of the class to locate and rescue each one. (As I set up this fiction for one group of 5th graders, several gave me quizzical looks. They actually believed me and couldn't understand why NASA was turning to a bunch of 11-year-olds to find their lost probes. I told them NASA had heard these kids were pretty sharp.) Unfortunately, the students have little information to work with: only a short video transmission from each probe just before it lost contact for good. With only this limited information, will the students be able to tell from which planet the probe sent the transmission?

Students tackle each probe, one at a time, based on the order you select. I play the transmission from the lost probe more than once. The first time, I tell students not to take any notes. Just watch and look for visual clues. Then we view it a second time, taking notes along the way. The visuals are all realistic. Students see what actual probes have captured on camera. Each expert is focused on different kinds of information which are dispersed throughout the transmission. Once the notes are gathered, each expert turns to his or her expert

It is a dynamic group experience.

...it's a beautiful, realistic journey.

I really love to push the fiction.

Interactive Video, Multimedia & All that Jazz

Each team consists of four experts __ an astronomer, a geologist, a meteorologist, and an historian.

booklet, which contains data on the planets. They look for matches. Is it a gas giant or a terrestrial planet? An inner planet or an outer one? What do we know about its geology or climate? What about past explorations? All students generate a list of possibilities, which they share with their teammates. Only by

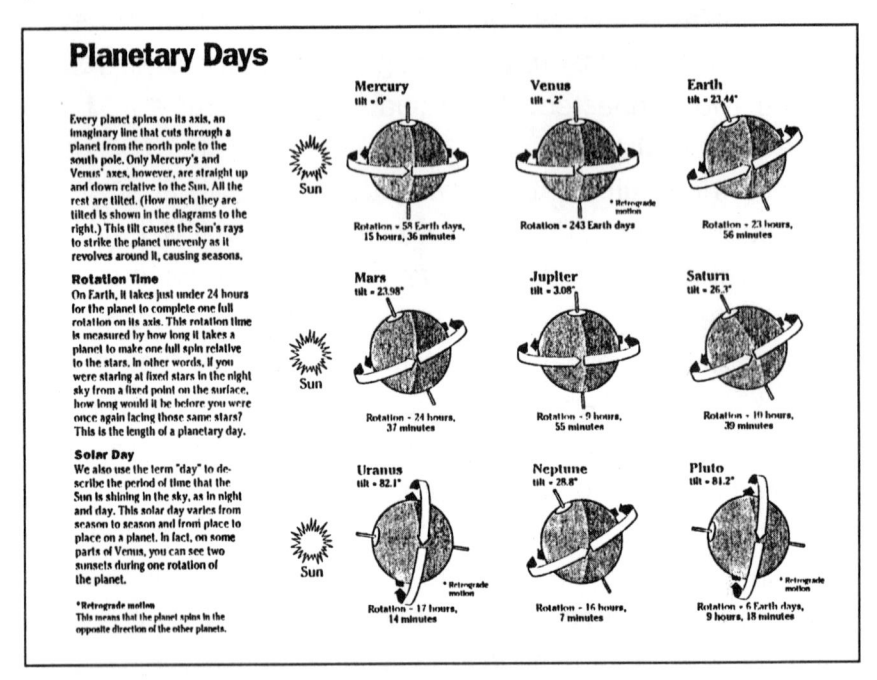

Planetary Days

Every planet spins on its axis, an imaginary line that cuts through a planet from the north pole to the south pole. Only Mercury's and Venus' axes, however, are straight up and down relative to the Sun. All the rest are tilted. (How much they are tilted is shown in the diagrams to the right.) This tilt causes the Sun's rays to strike the planet unevenly as it revolves around it, causing seasons.

Rotation Time
On Earth, it takes just under 24 hours for the planet to complete one full rotation on its axis. This rotation time is measured by how long it takes a planet to make one full spin relative to the stars. In other words, if you were staring at fixed stars in the night sky from a fixed point on the surface, how long would it be before you were once again facing those same stars? This is the length of a planetary day.

Solar Day
We also use the term "day" to describe the period of time that the Sun is shining in the sky, as in night and day. This solar day varies from season to season and from place to place on a planet. In fact, on some parts of Venus, you can see two sunsets during one rotation of the planet.

*Retrograde motion
This means that the planet spins in the opposite direction of the other planets.

Mercury tilt = 0° — Rotation = 58 Earth days, 15 hours, 36 minutes
Venus tilt = 2° — Rotation = 243 Earth days *Retrograde motion
Earth tilt = 23.44° — Rotation = 23 hours, 56 minutes
Mars tilt = 23.98° — Rotation = 24 hours, 37 minutes
Jupiter tilt = 3.08° — Rotation = 9 hours, 55 minutes
Saturn tilt = 26.3° — Rotation = 10 hours, 39 minutes
Uranus tilt = 82.1° — Rotation = 17 hours, 14 minutes *Retrograde motion
Neptune tilt = 28.8° — Rotation = 16 hours, 7 minutes
Pluto tilt = 81.2° — Rotation = 6 Earth days, 9 hours, 18 minutes

working together can they narrow the list down to the correct planet. I ask each group to give a recommendation with reasons. After some discussion, they agree on a planet. Traveling to that planet in search of the lost probe is expensive, so they had better be right. They don't want to waste money.

Once they arrive at the planet (and it's a beautiful, realistic journey), the students find that their mission is only half complete. There is another obstacle to overcome, which varies from planet to planet. The class can make contact with the lost probe, but the students can't pinpoint its exact location or figure out how to rescue it. They must select an appropriate rescue plan (there are four available for each planet) that will successfully recover the probe. But which plan? Fortunately, each probe comes equipped with a set of tools that can perform tests on the area surrounding it. Students use the tests (each one costs a small amount of money, much less than a rescue plan) to narrow their choices. Again, there's group debate. The temperature test will probably eliminate only one of the rescue plans while the surface analyzer will narrow it down to two possibilities. This second part of the mission requires a high level of deductive reasoning.

As you can see, *The Great Solar System Rescue* is above all a group experience. The video is intimately integrated into the activity, supporting the content by welcoming students into a world (actually a solar system) so difficult to capture with words alone.

The Wonderful Problems of Fizz & Martina and *The Great Solar System Rescue* are two examples of true multimedia, combining video, print and human communication. It's that last element that really makes multimedia worthwhile. After all, when you get right down to it, it's not interactive technology we seek, it's the *interactive classroom*. As we get bombarded by ever glitzier media and combinations of media, we can't forget that the most powerful medium for expression and understanding is already in the classroom. Technology should help us (teachers) exploit the incredible energy and emotion bottled up inside our students in ways that are practical and powerful. So as multimedia sweeps your eyes into the clouds, be sure to keep your heart in the classroom.

Human communication is what makes it all worthwhile.

Notes From The Field

Ideas from teachers who live in a one computer classroom

It's easy for me, or for any "outsider", to talk about what should happen in your classroom. It probably means much more to you to hear from those directly "in the field" that these kinds of activities can actually happen. In 1988 Tom Snyder Productions sponsored a contest looking for the best uses of a single computer in the classroom. The company received entries from creative teachers across the country. Their efforts and ideas are worth sharing (and many can be found scattered throughout this book). Some of the teachers described interesting ways to take existing software designed for use in the computer lab and apply it successfully in whole group instruction. A few teachers even described simple programs they had written for themselves. (By the way, in the same manner that my old housemate created a grading program specifically for me, you too can likely find someone in your school to write discrete applications for your particular needs.) Some of those pieces of software were obscure and difficult for a third party to follow. But who cares? These personal programs weren't developed for commercial sale. All that matters, is that they worked for the teachers who created them.

I'd thought you'd enjoy a couple of excerpts from those contest entries. Maybe they will inspire you. Maybe they will reassure you. In any case, I hope that you enjoy them.

From Tony Dufour, Mt. Pleasant, SC

The school day has started. Susan, Jeremy, Maurice, and Renee all walk in the classroom.

Don't trust me, listen to these people "in the field."

All that matters is that the program work for you.

A typical school day

Notes From The Field

"a school...where learning with, not from, computers occurs."

"...teacher and students are participating in the educational loop."

"The computer is placed on the teacher's desk..."

Maurice unpacks his bag, Susan puts her books in the desk, Jeremy places his lunch bag in the lunch cubby, and Renee sets the monitors in place for another day of school where computers are used in the learning process.

What you have just read does not take place in the future. It occurs in a school in South Carolina where learning with, not from, computers occurs. It is the one computer class. It happens everyday in 4-D, in Whitesides Elementary School, in Mt. Pleasant, South Carolina.

Through the use of two old black and white televisions, and one very portable Laser 128 personal computer, teacher and students are participating in the educational loop. They are both interacting with programs that were originally designed to be used as drill and practice in a computer lab setting. They both are exploring and discussing concerns that would have been ignored, with a student using the same program in the computer lab. An Education is taking place.

The design of the classroom setting is such that two very old black and white televisions (which were designated to be put in moth balls because of their "outdatedness") are placed in the front of the classroom so that every student is able to see them. The computer is placed on the teacher's desk, with a monochrome monitor, and connected to the two televisions using several "Y" cable connectors, 4 24" RCA cables, and one extension cord. An overhead projector is placed between the two "old monster monitors."

With all the correct connections and a student familiar with the computer keyboard, a class can begin. The teacher places himself near the overhead so that he can interact with each student, face to face. The program has been preset in the computer prior to the beginning of the class. This done so that any pre-teaching activities are completed, or any class centered discussions occur.

As mentioned before, any program can be class centered. It can be class centered, if the teacher has an understanding of group work, an understanding that more than one student should be involved, higher order thinking questions are asked, and the teacher responds to answers when answers are given.

In 4-D, the class is using this single computer for drill and practice of math facts (using MECC's *Mastering Math Series*). They are using this design to correct a student's composition paper (using Milliken's *Writing Workshop*). They are exploring variables in scientific experiments (using Broderbund's *Science Toolkit*). They are exploring the United States (using Tom Snyder Production's *National Inspirer*). But what they are really doing is learning beyond the single textbook.

In all of these learning situations, this teacher is staying within this loop of learning and doing it successfully with the use of one computer.

Single Subject Uses in the Classroom Using One Computer

Homework. Homework has been planned and placed on a designated homework disk before the start of the school week. At the end of each day, the designated fourth grader loads up the program and turns on the two monitors so that the students may write down their homework.

"The teacher places himself... so that he can interact with each student, face to face."

"...any program can be class centered."

"But what they are really doing is learning beyond the single textbook."

"This has had a fantastic effect on the response rate of homework..."

Notes From The Field

"...has perked up the student's attitude and understanding of word problems."

"...students are becoming explorers."

"Creative writing and ... *TimeLiner* go hand-in-hand."

This has had a fantastic effect on the response rate of homework that is completed.

Math. Total class involvement in solving word problems. Using Level Five of *McGraw Hill's Mathematics Problem Solving Courseware*, developed by Tom Snyder Productions, has perked up the students' attitude and understanding of word problems. Everybody is involved in solving the single problem and in determining which path to take in the adventure. (These are fourth graders doing the program.) They continue understanding math problems through drill and practice using a variety of drill and practice software.

Science. Science means exploring, and the students are becoming explorers. Each day a group of students measure the sun's daily light intensity, sidewalk temperature, and path across the sky using Broderbund's *Science Toolkit*. Using a 24' RCA cable, which is located outside the classroom, students in daily groups of five take and record these sun measurements. These findings are then used in graphing various points using MECC's and Weekly Reader's graphing programs.

English. Creative writing and Tom Snyder Productions' *TimeLiner* go hand-in-hand. The whole class has the opportunity to write a story as a class. Students are asked to think of a general type of story. They then get an opportunity to tell of an event that takes place in the story. This event is then placed on a time line and printed out. This time line is now an outline. The story can be written (or changed) as the class deems necessary.

Students also have their weekly compositions

recorded on a data disk by parent volunteers. The parents type the students' stories as they are written without correcting the mistakes. Students then volunteer to have their stories corrected by the class, using Milliken's *Writing Workshop*. Each correct story is then published in the class' weekly paper.

Social Studies. Students can explore the United States as a group. No longer do they have to do the work on their own and hope that they have the correct answer. Using *National Inspirer* students put to use the practical skills of social studies.

Reading. Students can review comprehension questions of stories that they read using Sunburst's literature series. This gives a new approach to an old skill of questioning comprehension. This also allows the teacher to rebound off one question and ask another.

All of the above activities are performed using one computer and two classroom monitors. A total integration of the computer as a teaching tool, not a teaching sitter.

From Paul Boling, Ft. Leavenworth, KS

I have an Apple IIc in my classroom and have used it to run programs which were already written to supplement my German textbook *Deutsch Aktuell* from EMC publishing. The natural problem, however, was that the whole class was not able to see it on the tiny monitor. I decided to solve my problem by purchasing a modulator from

"Each correct story is then published in the class' weekly paper."

"Using *National Inspirer* students put to use the practical skills of social studies."

"...a new approach to an old skill of questioning comprehension."

"...the computer as a teaching tool, not a teaching sitter."

Foreign language and math examples

Notes From The Field

> "This was a great move, but my next problem was that I now had to have my back to the class..."

> "...the class loved it!"

> "The applications for use of a word processor on the large screen TV are endless."

Radio Shack for $26 so I could bring up the program on a big screen TV, of which we have a number shared by the faculty. This was a great move, but my next problem was that I now had to have my back to the class somewhat so that I, too, could see the screen. Next, I installed a splitter on the back of the CPU so that I could run a cable both to the monitor and to the TV. The result is I can now face the class and look at the monitor while the class is seeing the same thing in color on the TV.

Trying it out for the first time this year, the class loved it! My students in the past always wanted to rush through the entire diskette of programs, but now they want to take time enough to even take notes! Word processing software with a choice of fonts, such as *MultiScribe* for the Apple or *Personal Newsletter*, makes it possible to display characters which do not lose their clarity when enlarged by the big screen TV. The applications for use of a word processor on the large screen TV are endless. For example, in the teaching of sentence construction, whether in a foreign language or in English, text can easily be switched around by using edit commands, and the various position of the parts of speech and meaning they convey in each of those positions can be discussed without having to re-write the sentence each time. Students can be called up to the computer to type in their renditions, the whole class can comment as to accuracy, other possibilities discussed, and appropriate corrections can then be easily made. Students enjoy seeing the possibilities, and manipulating things for it gives them a sense of power.

I also use this set-up in Algebra class as a reward for good behavior. I have *Alge-blaster*, which my students particularly enjoy, and other programs which I can boot up and have students type in the steps, after which the whole class can be called upon to verify the validity of each before the return key is pressed for entering. I have a program that graphs linear equations which shows very easily what happens to the slope and y-intercept when variables are changed. I can cover more possibilities because I don't have to constantly erase and reconstruct and the students are able to see immediately the results. They can experiment and check their homework — seeing visually on a graph what happens with the manipulation of variables. This is exciting to them — beyond my expectations by simply putting it all on the big screen TV!

Other possibilities might include bringing up study notes for review, with the added capability of revising or adding additional information without running out of space, a common problem with prior-prepared overhead transparencies or writing it on the blackboard. If the added material is saved to the disk, other classes taught later on in the day can be more easily kept together and the teacher can be sure that all receive the same information. (One problem I have experienced as a classroom teacher is that sometimes I forget to impart the same information to all my classes, because after a few hours I tend to forget what I have said in one class as opposed to another. In addition, often things get erased from the blackboard from hour to hour. Also different classes tend to pose different questions which would be beneficial to all, and I sometimes make false assumptions that I have already covered certain issues in one class when, in fact, it was brought

"Students enjoy seeing the possibilities..."

"I can cover more possibilities because I don't have to constantly erase and reconstruct..."

"One problem I have experienced... is that sometimes I forget to impart the same information to all my classes."

Notes From The Field

"Saving it to a data disk assures me of fair and equal treatment to all my classes."

"This has so much potential, I can hardly stand it!"

up in another. Saving it to a data disk assures me of fair and equal treatment to all my classes.) Another idea is to store teacher-prepared quizzes to a data disk which takes up much less space than an ordinary file and can be much more easily retrieved at a later time. Simply display it on the big TV screen or print out a hard copy. Also, change can easily be made without having to retype the whole thing. Using a program which allows you to form a data base of hundreds of test items and then randomly selects and formulates a test is a tremendous tool as well. Virtually every class could have a different battery of questions on the same day. Just be careful to run a hard copy for each so there is no confusion in grading. Test items can easily be revised, edited, and updated as necessary. This has so much potential, I can hardly stand it! Classroom management will never be the same!

Epilogue

It's happening. You can see for yourself that the computer and other technologies are cramming their way into classrooms across the country. Each technology's impact on the schools, however, is far from inevitable. As these devices become increasingly available, you have the opportunity to take the lead in the "revolution." Steer it in the direction you want it to go. The ultimate success or failure of interactive technology in education depends on you anyway. So don't be an idle passenger who's just going along for the ride. Get yourself into the driver's seat. The teachers are the key implementers of education in our country, and if they — meaning you — refuse to accept the challenge that faces them, then the effort, like so many previous reforms, will die.

The ultimate success or failure of interactive technology in education depends on you.

Some Aides for Sharing Ideas

I encourage you to reproduce the illustrations and charts on the following pages and use them to share this vision of the one computer classroom. Make your own "scintillating, graphically compelling overheads" to help convince your colleagues to include teachers in the distribution of powerful resources in the school. Putting the computer into the hands of the teacher makes sense. We have to think of ourselves as professionals deserving of professional tools. The computer is one of those tools.

8 Tips For Beginning Computer Using Teachers

1. Take the computer to where you work.

2. Don't worry about breaking anything.
Be bold. Have a good time. What do you do when film breaks showing a movie? You can handle it.

3. Start easy.
You don't need to be a programmer to use the computer. If you have the time and access to machinery, just write a letter or try averaging your grades on the computer. If access is limited, start with a package that's classroom ready. Boot it up and give it a shot.

4. Be patient.
Anything new takes some initial investment.

5. Don't be afraid to seek help.
Use colleagues and the computer coordinator. There's nothing to be embarrassed about. Think how often you tell your students to seek help if they need it.

6. Keep it on your turf.
Whether working in the classroom or the computer lab, remember that you are in charge. Look for what fits and supports your goals.

7. Remain skeptical.
You probably already are skeptical, and you should be, so long as you maintain an open mind. Computers aren't good merely for their own sake.

8. Look for programs that make life easier for you.
Start with what you hate to do and see if the computer can help.

5 Issues To Consider Before Using Computers in Schools

As teachers are pushed toward computer use, we must be sensitive to a number of issues:

1. existing pressures on time and energy

teachers have a lot to do already. Besides teaching, they have administrative duties, monitorials, paper work, grading, lesson development, student club advising, and more. And at the same time as they are being pressured to integrate computers into their classrooms, they may also be pushed to implement critical thinking and cooperative learning, to raise test scores and improve basic skills. If the computer is just "one more thing," they will probably resist.

2. support within the school/department

exciting teachers about new ideas or new technologies without giving the support to follow-up is asking for frustration. Consider where a teacher lives and the resources currently available. Do teachers have access to the basic tools of their trade, let alone a computer? Is the school responsive to their needs? And what are the teachers' perceptions?

3. professional priorities

how high do computers rank on the list of professional growth priorities for each teacher? Are some more interested in gaining new content mastery in the discipline? Are others heading toward administrative positions? Are some merely biding their time?

4. self-esteem and confidence

as a group, teachers are an incredibly insecure lot. Given a history of low pay and low regard, that low self-esteem is not surprising. But whatever the cause, that situation creates a fairly risk-averse crowd. Teachers are not encouraged to take chances. They are rewarded for control and stability. Like students, they need reassurance and confidence to go forward with change.

5. knowledge of the machines

it's easy for experts to assume their audience knows more than they really do. The computer may seem like old hat to many of you, but it's still new to a number of teachers.

10 Tips For Computer Coordinators

1. Make the technology truly accessible to the teachers.
It's not enough to open up the computer lab after school. Accessibility doesn't mean having to squeeze into chairs made for fourth graders on your own time. Consider where teachers do their work. Is it in their classrooms? The department office? The dining room table at home? Do what you can to make the computer available in their space and in their time. Let computers go out overnight and over the weekend. Let teachers take them over the summer. Steal one from the lab and stick in the department office.

2. Real access includes time.
Do what you can to liberate teachers from administrative duties to give them time to experiment with the technology you're pushing. Relieving teachers of class time isn't always a benefit. They still have to prepare lessons and hold their students accountable, and they usually have to make up the time elsewhere. And many good teachers don't like to leave their classes.

3. Don't ask teachers to do things that make their lives more difficult.
That's a choice they have to make on their own for themselves. Otherwise, you only build resentment.

4. Give teachers tools that support what they do.
• if the access is there offer word processors and grading programs. Point teachers to uses that are personally rewarding and address activities they don't like anyway and can do on their own time.
• if teachers have little access to work on their own, then focus them towards ready-to-use, non-disruptive software programs. Give them something they can use in the classroom immediately with virtually no preparation. How many teachers preview films in the classroom? It's often their only opportunity.

5. Build a partnership with the teachers.
Attend in-services together; make plans and experiment with new programs jointly. To some extent, you've got to know what they know. Attending trainings with teachers in tow creates opportunities for you to turn and say, "See, that's what I was telling you. Here's how we can do this." It's great. Nothing like striking while the iron is hot.

6. Involve administrators and department heads in your efforts.

These folks have the power to relieve teachers of other obligations and to take quick action. They also have the authority to downplay other pressures teachers might be feeling, like raising test scores, covering large amounts of material, or solving community drug problems. Their presence allows you to do something right away.

7. Strive for fast follow-up.

If a program generates some interest, make it available as quickly as possible. The longer you wait, the more enthusiasm and excitement will wane. And set goals for use, or at least for examination. Establish dates and time for follow-up meetings, phone calls, or letters to see how things are going. Subtle pressure goes a long way.

8. Be patient.

Treat learning teachers as you do learning students. Consider individual learning styles, personal interests. As with any students, it often takes time for new ideas to take hold.

9. Be realistic, even skeptical.

Don't "pie in the sky" your colleagues. Acknowledge the realities of their situation, and don't promise what you can't deliver. New technology may look gorgeous and may dazzle the viewer, but can teachers really use it?

10. Don't push technology for its own sake.

My Life Before Computers

The Unfulfilled Promise of Computers

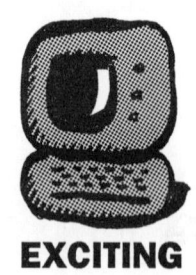

EXCITING

POWERFUL

The Two Sides of Teaching

CHARMING

The Management   **The Craft**

Guaranteed to fill all your teaching needs!!

ENGAGING

INTERACTIVE

Where are the Computers?

LABS

The lab is great for special projects, but it's not where you live. Like the library, it's a shared resource in the school.

RESOURCE ROOMS

The resource area works well for one or two students using the computer under the guidance of a teacher, but again, it's not the classroom.

What's Wrong with this Picture?

The Computer in the Back of the Classroom

While one student played with the computer, the rest of the class wondered why they weren't.

Welcome to the One Computer Classroom

THE PROMISE OF COMPUTERS

Two Sides of Teaching

The Craft **The Management**

Can the Computer Help?

THE PROMISE OF COMPUTERS

Elements of Successful Classroom Technology

Support of Teacher Control
Use of the technology must <u>not</u> make the teacher's management task <u>more</u> difficult.

Pedagogic Flexibility
The technology must support the various ways teachers teach.

Accessibility
Teachers must have access to it where they work, both inside and outside the classroom.

THE PROMISE OF COMPUTERS

What Can a Good Teacher Do With a Computer?

Manage responsibilities and paperwork

Make dazzling presentations

Lead incredible discussions

Manage dynamic cooperative learning activities

Inspire enlightening self-discovery

Permission granted to copy for educational uses only. Copyright © 1991 Tom Snyder Productions, Inc.

THE COMPUTER CAN HELP

Manage Responsibilities and Paperwork

- Ease the burden of redundant administrivia
- Manage student records, grades, and attendance
- Generate tests, worksheets, handouts, and displays
- Produce reports, letters, and notes
- Create and modify curriculum
- Increase teacher professionalism

THE COMPUTER CAN HELP

Make Dazzling Presentations

- **Illustrate ideas and concepts**
- **Manage and organize information**
- **Assist in classroom management**
- **Encourage student participation**
- **Enliven demonstrations**

THE COMPUTER CAN HELP

Lead incredible discussions

- **Prompt discussion**
- **Promote debate**
- **Manage information**
- **Support role playing**
- **Create a compelling context**
- **Enhance drama and excitement**

THE COMPUTER CAN HELP

Manage dynamic cooperative learning activities

- Disseminate information
- Pace group movement
- Distribute responsibilities
- Enforce group interdependence
- Involve individual students as part of team
- Prompt cross-group interactions

THE COMPUTER CAN HELP

Inspire enlightening self-discovery

- **Provide access to information**
- **Offer tools for organizing and manipulating data**
- **Engage exploration in a compelling context**
- **Display content in alternative forms**

Related, Historical and Contemporary Reading

Anderson, Charnel. *Technology in American Education, 1650-1900.* Washington, DC: GPO, 1962.

Cuban, Larry. *Teachers and Machines.* New York: Teachers College Press, 1986.

Dockterman, David A. and Tom Snyder. *Bringing the Computer into Your Classroom.* Cambridge, MA: Tom Snyder Productions, 1987.

Dockterman, David A. *Tools for Teachers: An Historical Analysis of Classroom Technology.* Doctoral thesis Harvard Graduate School of Educationa, 1988.

Hampel, Robert L. *The Last Little Citadel: American High Schools Since 1940.* Boston: Houghton Mifflin Company, 1986.

Herndon, James. *Notes from a Schoolteacher.* New York: Simon and Schuster, 1985.

Jackson, Philip W. *The Teacher and the Machine.* Pittsburgh: University of Pittsburgh Press, 1968.

Kidder, Tracy. *Among Schoolchildren.* Boston: Houghton Mifflin Company, 1989.

Neustadt, Richard E. and Ernest R. May. *Thinking in Time.* New York: St. Martin's Press, 1981.

Oettinger, Anthony G. *Run, Computer, Run. The Mythology of Educational Innovation.* Cambridge, MA: Harvard University Press, 1969.

Papert, Seymour. *Mindstorms.* New York: Basic Books, 1980.

Powell, Arthur G., Eleanor Farrar, and David K. Cohen. *The Shopping Mall High School.* Boston: Houghton Mifflin Company, 1985.

Saettler, Paul. *A History of Educational Technology.* New York: McGraw-Hill Book Company, 1968.

Sizer, Theodore. *Horace's Compromise.* Boston: Houghton Mifflin Company, 1985.

Snyder, Tom and David Dockterman. *"Getting to Aha!"* in Electronic Learning, Vol. 3, No. 8, 1983.

Snyder, Tom and Jane Palmer. *In Search of the Most Amazing Thing.* Reading, MA: Addison-Wesley Publishing Company, Inc., 1986.

Weizenbaum, Joseph. *Computer Power and Human Reason.* San Francisco: W.H. Freeman and Company, 1976.

Great Teachers!

We've got even more great stuff that can help YOU! Use the order form below or call us toll-free at

1-800-342-0236

The Complete In-Service Workshop Kit

Here's the most cost-effective way to train your staff and get your school excited about using computers. Whether you're wondering what to do with one computer in your classroom, have access to a computer lab and never use it, or are an experienced computer user looking for new ideas, our workshop kit has the answers. It offers practical suggestions, motivating activities, outlines, reproducibles and tips from the field.

Includes: Great Workshops Guide • Great Teaching in the One Computer Classroom Book • The One Computer Classroom Video • Overhead Transparencies **$49.95**

...Or we can come to you!

We even offer on-site workshops with one of our highly praised in-service presenters! For a brochure with pricing and scheduling information, contact:
Tom Snyder Productions, In-Service Program, 90 Sherman St., Cambridge, MA 02140
Or Call: 1-800-342-0236

Free! TSP Catalog!

Our terrific 40-page, full color catalog is *the* resource for great teachers. Find out all about our award-winning products for the one (or one-plus) computer classroom. **FREE!**

Great Workshops The TSP In-Service Guide

This delightfully written book contains everything you need to conduct a first-rate computer workshop in your school. From relating to your audience to connecting a computer to a TV, to designing the perfect workshop, it's all here – even overhead transparencies! You get three detailed model workshops:
• The One Computer Classroom
• The Computer in the Social Studies
• Critical Thinking, Cooperative Learning and the Computer.
Plus you get step-by step instructions for designing your own customized workshops. **$49.95**

Great Teaching in the One Computer Classroom

This popular book is full of practical and inspirational ideas. Spread the word by ordering copies for your colleagues! **$19.95**

The One Computer Classroom Video

Includes: Video outline - useful presentation outlines and information to share with your audience • Video Presentation Information - valuable tips and tidbits • Video Catalog of 25 TSP titles. Try it free for 30 days! **$19.95**

Free 30-day loan!

Product	Price	Qty	Cost
The TSP Catalog	FREE!		
The Complete In-Service Workshop Kit	$49.95		
Great Workshops: The In-Service Guide	$19.95		
Great Teaching in the One Computer Classroom	$19.95		
The One Computer Classroom Video	$19.95		
The One Computer Classroom Video (FREE 30-day loan)			
Subtotal			
Tax (MA residents add 5%)			
8% Shipping and Handling			
Total			

Ship to: Name _____
Title _____
School _____
Address _____
City _____ State ___ Zip ___
Phone _____

Billing: Payment enclosed: ❑ Check ❑ Visa ❑ Mastercard
PO# _____ account# _____
Signature _____ exp. date _____

CALL 1-800-342-0236 TODAY!

A peek at our fan mail...

"TSP software would always be my first choice. It is excellent, well written, well documented, can be used in a variety of ways and has great educational value!"
• Susan Tallman, Pearl River High School
  Pearl River, NY

. . . .

"The philosophy of TSP is unique and I appreciate the thought and preparation put into each of the programs I've seen."
• Sara Shein, East Prarie School
  Skokie, IL

. . . .

"Outstanding software! Students love it!"
• Carla Oster, Standing Rock College
  Fort Yates, ND

. . . .

"I have been pleased with EVERY piece of software purchased from you."
• Susan Simons, Center Road School
  Vernon, CT

"If it's a TSP, it's so exciting, educationally sound, and easily fits into curriculum areas. Products are curriculum driven and designed to enrich any teachers program."
• Joan Hamilton, Emerson School
  Bolton, MA

. . . .

"I have never been disappointed with any of your products. I feel that I can purchase your materials sight unseen and know that they will be easy to use, dependable, and right on target for the curriculum."
• Cindy Servi, Apopka High School
  Apopka, FL

. . . .

"We are very pleased with the Tom Snyder packages. They are high quality educational programs and come with great teaching suggestions."
• Michelle Churma, South Euclid, OH

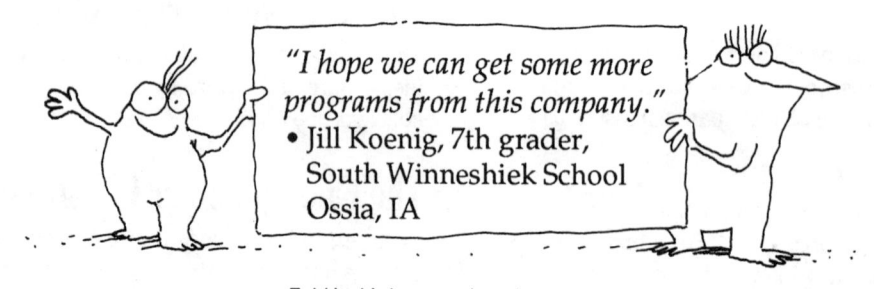

"I hope we can get some more programs from this company."
• Jill Koenig, 7th grader,
  South Winneshiek School
  Ossia, IA

Fold in thirds, tape closed

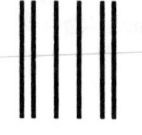

BUSINESS REPLY MAIL
FIRST CLASS PERMIT NO. 03257 CAMBRIDGE MA

POSTAGE WILL BE PAID BY ADDRESSEE

TOM SNYDER PRODUCTIONS, INC.
90 SHERMAN STREET - DEPT WB
CAMBRIDGE, MA 02140

NO POSTAGE
NECESSARY
IF MAILED
IN THE
UNITED STATES